Counselling skills
IN SOCIAL WO

361·06

q

For Deborah, Charlotte and Matthew
Helena, Tony and Joy
Lily, Cliff and Antony
and especially for Roy, with much love

Counselling skills
IN SOCIAL WORK PRACTICE

Janet Seden

Open University Press
Buckingham · Philadelphia

Open University Press
Celtic Court
22 Ballmoor
Buckingham
MK18 1XW

email: enquiries@openup.co.uk
world wide web: www.openup.co.uk

and
325 Chestnut Street
Philadelphia, PA 19106, USA

First Published 1999
Reprinted 2000, 2001

A catalogue record of this book is available from the British Library

ISBN   0 335 19968 2 (pb)   0 335 19969 0 (hb)

Library of Congress Cataloging-in-Publication Data
Seden, Janet. 1947–
    Counselling skills in social work practice / Janet Seden.
        p.   cm.
    Includes bibliographical references.
    ISBN 0–335–19969–0. – ISBN 0–335–19968–2 (pbk.)
    1. Social service–Great Britain.   2. Social case work–Great
Britain.   3. Counseling–Great Britain.   4. Counselor and client–
Great Britain.   I. Title.
HV245.S42   1999
361'.06–dc21   98–55534
                                                                        CIP

Typeset by Graphicraft Limited, Hong Kong
Printed in Great Britain by The Cromwell Press, Trowbridge

Contents

Preface

This book is one of a series of books published by Open University Press which considers the relationship between counselling skills and the professional concerns of a specific group, in this case social workers. The volume is therefore organized around the six core qualifying practice competences required for the revised Diploma in Social Work (CCETSW 1995). These competences, when examined, encapsulate some key themes, theories and methods for social work practice which can be found in the past and present social work literature. The knowledge, skills and values thus articulated provide a firm basis for social work activity, although the ideologies, legislative mandates and societal expectations of practitioners change.

The general theoretical and methodological material used in this volume is drawn from the writer's own experience, research, teaching material and a commissioned literature review, 'Contributing to the development framework for the needs-led assessment of children and their families', recently completed for the Department of Health. Thanks for agreement to draw on this work are registered here, as well as thanks to all those who mentored its production.

This book, however, is chiefly about the application of counselling skills to social work practice. I have been teaching basic and advanced skills to counselling and social work students for some years now, focusing on a generic skills base for social work students rather than on counselling practice. Social work students have always been motivated to link skills to their everyday practice experience. Their feedback on the interview skills sequence is consistently positive and always includes comment on the usefulness of the live, supervised practice of communication skills. I have therefore aimed to balance social work methods, theories and values with counselling skills in examples of practitioner work in this book. Counselling skills are seen as tools to underpin a range of theories, methods and frameworks for social work.

In social workers' everyday work a synthesis of knowledge, values and skills working together for effective service delivery is the hallmark of good practice. However, I also believe that the client as a unique person should always be at the centre of best practice. The practitioner's contribution to the client's life must be communicated clearly, undertaken in supportive partnership and carried out with conscious consent, as far as is humanly and legally possible. Counselling skills can be used in order to achieve this process of intervention. Relationship is still the basis for professional interaction provided individuals are respected, rather than pathologized, and structural difficulties are fully appreciated. Frameworks for tasks change, but attention to good process is always necessary, especially because of concern to avoid discrimination and harm in what we as social workers do when we intervene in the lives of others.

On a stylistic note, I have referred to clients, service users, recipients of services and customers to denote those people with whom social workers engage. This is deliberate, as while client remains perhaps the most accurate term, this is a matter of professional debate. Currently the term 'service user' is found most often in social work writing and 'client' in counselling literature. None of the alternatives to client seem to encapsulate accurately enough the whole of what people's transactions with social workers are about. Likewise, social worker, worker and practitioner are interchangeably used to describe the professional in action.

Social work has been subject to media and moral panic from society in recent years, because it appears either that 'too little' was done to prevent a tragedy, or that 'too much' was done and civil rights were breached. No profession is omniscient, and social workers and their managers can and do make misjudgements. However, I wish to focus on the fact that day in, day out, on a national basis, social workers are carrying out their tasks in a caring, competent and effective way which rarely seems to be publicly acknowledged. Many of the interventions made are not glamorous, dramatic or 'worthy' of headlines in papers, but they are important, essential and of meaning to the recipients of the service. Moving from home to residential care or hospital, having difficulties with your parents, losing a child, liberty, income or citizenship are some of the serious life events where social workers become involved. I hope the practice examples show social workers who are committedly carrying out their everyday mandated tasks in an effective and caring way, with children, families and adults, in the range of organizations where they are employed.

Likewise, the search for the 'new' is often promoted at the expense of evaluating what we know and developing advanced skill in what is well established. Counselling and counselling skills are now embedded as a means of improving communication in human services organizations. Supervised reflective practice and continued training are what keep these skills effective. Much social work is about detailed and minute transactions between people, where counselling skills are the most precise tool for communicating well. Often very essential work is undertaken with marginalized, vulnerable or disadvantaged groups, through patient attention to both communication and the actions which may follow.

The practice examples are just that. They are not case studies, but are drawn from real situations, reworked and rewritten for publication. They are included in order to demonstrate practical use of the counselling skills described. As I worked with this material, I realized that these are fairly typical of the kinds of social work practice which both use counselling skills to facilitate intervention and offer brief supportive counselling as part of the process of the work. There is no attempt to cover all aspects of practice; however, I hope there is sufficient to illustrate how counselling skills are relevant in underpinning a broad raft of standard social work within permitted legal and organizational mandates. The examples used are drawn from the work of beginning and experienced practitioners who hold recognized social work qualifications. Practice is included from children and family, community care, adult, criminal justice and voluntary sector practice. Context shapes every piece of work, but the choices that are made about process distinguish best practice from basic bureaucratic competence.

Some busy practitioners will say that they are no longer able to allow sufficient time for listening to people's needs. They might say that the social work task is only an administrative and functional one. In this book I take a different view of practice and this is why I have written it. I would say that good organizational and administrative skills are essential to social work practice, and legal requirements must be met properly, but:

- busy people need to be more skilled in basic counselling skills to achieve accurate communication in the limited time allocated;
- clients are entitled to articulate their own perceived needs and to be heard as a person by someone who offers them respect, understanding and cultural sensitivity;
- services that are offered should be agreed by recipients and viewed by them as relevant;
- working plans which are too rushed and imposed on people are poor practice and quickly break down, and in the long term this is more costly and less effective than taking a little more time and care over listening, checking and responding in the initial stages of interviewing and assessment;
- social work remains an activity where the interpersonal transaction between the person who needs a service and the person who responds is highly significant in contributing to creating and maintaining an effective outcome;
- the user, and his or her strengths, views and motivation, should be at the centre of all social work activity as much as can be congruent with legal and ethical practice.

Acknowledgements are due, for assistance and permission for free use of their work, to, in alphabetical order: Kimberley Absalom, Pauline Anstead, Juliet Bewley, Julie Brooks, Lorraine Chapman, Toni Fox, Sandra Holyoake, Elizabeth Lawrence, Liz McKenzie, Sarah Morris, David Neville, Sarah Orgill, Moira Phillips, Arlene Price, Pamela Shenton, Chris Shotton, Andy Smith, Martin Shaw, Richard Taylor, Martyn Vail and Claire Wilkinson. The merits of the examples are theirs, the demerits entirely my own. Other acknowledgements are within the text.

Thanks are also due to those who offered work which could not be included and those who completed the questionnaire mentioned in Chapter 1. Acknowledgement should also be made here of the invaluable and patient assistance of the series editor, Michael Jacobs, the encouragement of Professor Jane Aldgate and the support of other academic, professional and student colleagues at the Leicester University School of Social Work.

Janet Seden
Leicester 1999

Chapter 1

Relevant skills for social work practice

Mrs Andrews, aged 67, was trying to obtain some help for her elderly relative Mr Yelland, aged 87, who lived several miles away. He was becoming frail and less able to manage to care for himself, needing assistance with washing, dressing, shopping and cooking. His doctor had suggested a home carer could be provided through social services. Mrs Andrews was very concerned about Mr Yelland, especially as she was caring for her sick husband, aged 71. This meant she could not visit her uncle, who had no other relative nearby and had been 'like a father' to her. She consulted the local advice centre and was given the telephone number for the adult services team which applied to her uncle's home. She phoned feeling rather anxious, and although the worker who took her call was courteous and efficient, he requested information by a series of rapid questions. Mrs Andrews was informed that a referral had been taken, that a telephone call would be made to ascertain if Mr Yelland wanted a visit and that someone would go and see him.

The call ended and Mrs Andrews began to worry whether she had done the right thing. She had managed to pass on the information but now felt upset. She had been unable to say how concerned she felt, or to explain how difficult it was for her uncle, who had always been well and independent, not to be able to manage simple tasks. She had not been able to share how worried she was that he was forgetting things, that he might mind about a visit or that he was not caring for himself properly. She wondered how he would feel about a stranger visiting his home and what was behind all the questions the social worker asked. She had a sleepless night worrying about what she had done.

Meanwhile, in another city, Mrs Dalgleish, aged 67, was trying to obtain some help for her elderly relative Mr Ennis, aged 85, who lived several miles away. He too was becoming frail and unable to care for himself. He needed assistance with washing, dressing, shopping and cooking. She was very concerned about him, especially as she was caring for her sick husband, aged 71, and could not visit Mr Ennis, who had no relative any nearer. She consulted the local advice centre and was given the telephone number for the adult services team which applied to her uncle's home. She telephoned feeling rather anxious. The worker at the end of the telephone was courteous and efficient, but after asking for some basic information asked her how she thought her uncle would react to the referral. Mrs Dalgleish felt relieved to be able to share her concerns.

She was helped by the worker acknowledging the difficulty of this potential change for Mr Ennis. It was also helpful that, beginning to feel that the worker understood, she could share that she was also concerned about her uncle's forgetfulness and lack of care for himself. The worker explored these concerns and finished by offering to read back what he had written down so that Mrs Dalgleish could be sure it was correct. The worker also checked what times of day might be best to call Mr Ennis, whether he was expecting to hear from social services and whether he could easily use the telephone. This attention to detail and checking back was reassuring. Mrs Dalgleish was informed that a referral had been taken, that a telephone call would be made to ascertain that Mr Ennis did want a visit, that someone would go and see him and that she would be contacted about the outcome. The call ended and Mrs Dalgleish began to feel it would be all right. She had done the right thing. She called her uncle to let him know what would be happening.

At one time, it would have been thought obvious that social workers use counselling and casework in their tasks (Perlman 1957; Biestek 1961; Hollis 1964; Mayer and Timms 1970; Roberts and Nee 1970). The current preoccupation with quasi-markets, commissioners, providers, resources and outcomes might lead the present observer to the conclusion that such skills are no longer needed. Social workers employed in local authorities may have entered the profession thinking that they would focus on the kind of assistance given by counsellors to their clients. They now find themselves overwhelmed by work of a more bureaucratic and directive kind, which meets the requirements of the legal mandates of social services. Meanwhile, they make referrals and commission a range of specialist services, many in the voluntary and private sector, including some which offer counselling based on the old notions of casework. Some workers still make therapeutic relationships and provide a direct counselling service (Barnes 1990).

However, the relationship between counselling and social work has always been more complex and interactive than this simple division of functions suggests. Workers trained in the 1960s and early 1970s were grounded in casework principles based on largely psychodynamic theoretical underpinnings. Since those times social work training has moved in other diverse directions, embracing behavioural and ecological theories and a range of derivative practice methods. Through radical and Marxist approaches and a re-examination of values it has reclaimed the original preoccupation with social inequalities, injustice and social exclusion, despite a climate of resource constraint.

By the mid-nineties, it seemed that casework appeared to be less prioritized than empowerment ideologies and functionalism. The idea of a therapeutic relationship appeared to be subsumed to legislative priorities. Some social workers might now go as far as to argue that counselling skills are no longer relevant to social work practice and that the focus on the struggles of the individual is pathologizing. In particular they are concerned that any skills used in practice are congruent with the value base prescribed for newly qualifying social workers by the Central Council for Education and Training in Social Work (CCETSW), which set the standards for the new Diploma in Social Work (formerly CQSW) in 1991 and the revised Diploma in 1995.

However, like social work practice, counselling has developed since the 1970s and 1980s. It has diversified, expanded and developed from its psychoanalytic origins. While psychodynamic work is still a major theoretical approach in counselling literature, other approaches flourish, such as person-centred, behavioural, cognitive and Gestalt. There has been a re-evaluation of counselling practice and its relevance to women, black people, lesbian, gay and bisexual people, younger and older people and those who are disabled. Counselling training, like social work training, has re-examined its ideologies and practice as society's attitudes and values have changed. Paternalistic and discriminatory ideologies and models have been challenged and approaches re-evaluated. Therefore, much theoretical knowledge and many skills or ways of working from the two literatures can still be mutually enriching.

At the same time, there is some lack of clarity about the boundaries between the two activities. At one extreme all direct work with clients in social work agencies is labelled counselling, while at the other some social workers regard counselling as entirely a matter for specialist referral or the commissioning of services. Both extremes fail to negotiate the boundaries between the two disciplines adequately. The reality is that social workers in some situations take on a counselling role, and that counselling skills can be applied to a variety of social work tasks. The boundary confusion is not helped by the fact that an individual social worker may take on a number of roles in relation to a particular person, so that the counselling element of the working contract needs to be distinguished, clarified and contracted openly in relation to the overall package of work being undertaken (Hill and Meadows 1990).

The historical and current interaction is described and discussed by Judith Brearley (1991), who traces the ways in which social work and counselling have intertwined and influenced each other in terms of skills, knowledge and values, and how the two disciplines have also developed distinct identities and training pathways. She appraises the uses of counselling in social work and writes:

> the Barclay report identified counselling as one of the two main activities of social workers, the other being social care planning, and the report acknowledged the interlocking nature of these activities. The particular, perhaps unique, challenge faced by social workers is to offer counselling in a way that is integrated appropriately with a variety of other approaches in the overall work with a given client often within the same interview.
>
> (Brearley 1991: 30)

She continues:

> A logical categorization of the counselling dimensions of social work would therefore be as follows:
>
> • counselling skills underpinning the whole range of social work tasks;
> • counselling as a significant component of the work, carried out in conjunction with other approaches;
> • counselling as a major explicit part of the job description.

This book is primarily concerned with examining the relationship between counselling skills and social work practice – the first two of Brearley's categories. My own background as a social worker, social work lecturer, counsellor and counselling trainer makes me acutely aware of both the commonalities and differences of approach at a practice level between social workers and counsellors in the application of skills to their work.

I am aware that social workers are often unclear about the counselling skills that apply to social work and what the major specialist counselling approaches offer to clients. I am also aware that counsellors can be unduly critical of the legally mandated and bureaucratic task-centred parts of social work, without appreciating the counselling and other interpersonal skills needed to facilitate these complex and difficult human interactions. When one is operating across the two professional areas it is clear that there is overlap in practice skills, shared values and shared knowledge, as well as differences about how professional mandates and ethics determine the content of the facilitating work with people.

In this book I seek to identify the way certain skills facilitate and enhance social work practice, in its current legal and ideological frameworks. My assumption is that while the skills of listening, responding and relatedness may in themselves appear neutral, once they are utilized by any individual or agency, they are informed by that person's or organization's value and knowledge base and this will affect the outcomes. Thus similar skills are used in different ways and to different ends depending on what the worker and client have agreed. This is also significantly affected by the context in which the work takes place.

The lack of clarity about the role of counselling in social work practice is perhaps an outcome of psychodynamic case work having a symbiotic relationship with the newly emerging social work profession, which in its early days was seeking to identify which areas of expertise distinguished it from other professional activities. This was most clearly the case in the early part of the twentieth century when casework literature from America dominated social work. The dominance of social casework and its effectiveness were questioned in the 1970s and challenged by Marxist, behavioural radical and other approaches in the 1980s. In particular, the more politicized approaches led social work to redefine itself by ideology as much as methodology. At the same time, the profession became wary of those psychoanalytical approaches which appeared to pathologize or even blame the individual by addressing the inner psychic world rather than the external realities of oppressions acting upon the person living in a discriminatory society.

In the 1990s it became possible to assert that the distinctiveness of social work might be identified more by a value base within legal mandates than by particular sets of methods. It is impossible, therefore, to think about the place of counselling skills in social work without considering them in relation to the current prescribed value base and the accompanying core practice competences against which new trainees are now tested in order to gain the Revised Diploma in Social Work (1995). These define current understandings of social work activity.

It is very important to stress the importance of legal mandates in defining the boundaries of social work practice. It is the law which carries the values and philosophies that influence society's approaches to the care and control of some citizens by others. Developments in legislation and associated political ideologies have been crucial in shaping policies and practice during the late 1990s. Three key pieces of legislation (Children Act 1989, NHS and Community Care Act 1990, Criminal Justice Act 1991) have dominated the thinking of the profession about role and function. The competence model has dominated the assessment of entrants to the profession. The ideologies of markets and management are defining frameworks for practice in new and significant ways (Taylor-Gooby and Lawson 1993). As these three factors become embedded, space for considering theories, methods and models afresh is leading to a spate of new publishing about how tasks are accomplished through the social work process. Methods are being reappraised for current applicability (Doel and Marsh 1992; Thompson 1995; Trowell and Bower 1996).

Counselling has been disserviced and misunderstood within social work, in the sense that the word is often used without any real clarity about its meaning. This has been reflected in much social work literature, ever since the Barclay Report, which included counselling as a function of social work, but without providing any further definition. It can be assumed that personal support and listening on casework principles is what is meant, but to anyone with modern counselling training this is too simplistic. Counselling, like social work, is not simply one way of working. It includes several major schools of thought and practice, with differing theoretical underpinnings. It is important to stress that the range of approaches to counselling practice is diverse, as the literature can demonstrate (Mearns and Thorne 1988; Corey 1997; Egan 1990; Jacobs 1985, 1996; Davies and Neal 1996; Lago and Thompson 1996; Heron 1997).

Given the variety of possible approaches, counselling as a generic term can be very misleading. It is important that service users know what is being offered and the premises on which a particular service is based, particularly its ethics and values. Therefore, if social workers are commissioning counselling services for their clients, they will need to know, at least at a minimal level, how the different therapeutic schools operate. If they have no such knowledge they are not in a position to enable their service users to make an informed choice about which kinds of therapy are on offer and which they might find the most helpful. Social workers might in some circumstances advise a service user to think carefully before entering a complex therapeutic process for which he or she may not be suited.

It is still rightly assumed that some counselling is done by social workers, but a recent study of beginning practitioners' readiness for practice (undertaken by Marsh and Triseliotis in 1996) indicates that social work skills is an area where the respondents would have liked more training. Fifty-one per cent said that too little time on their course had been spent on social work skills, by which they meant those techniques and actions by which tasks are processed, including communication skills. 'Counselling approaches and interpersonal skills appear to be widely taught' (Marsh and Triseliotis 1996b: 52), but students apparently remain unclear about how these relate to the pragmatic tasks undertaken in social services departments. The study also found that the students interviewed split off theory from the agency task and reported that this link was not made well by teachers, 'The reality for many respondents was that the actual application of theory to practice was very poorly done and proved to be one of the weakest parts of the course' (Marsh and Triseliotis 1996b: 60).

The authors describe the type of counselling taught as largely relying on Rogerian perspectives or Egan's goal-centred psychodynamic model:

> The definition of counselling itself varies widely, depending on the perspective from which it is being defined and practised. Approaches can range from total non-directiveness at one end of the continuum (if such a thing is at all possible) to degrees of direction and even challenge at the other end. In fact it is difficult to see how any sort of social work activity or interaction can take place without some form of 'counselling' taking place, unless the word is reserved exclusively for some kind of esoteric/therapeutic approach.
> (Marsh and Triseliotis 1996b: 54)

The study provides more evidence of the lack of clarity in social work training around the differences between counselling skills for social work practice, specialist counselling approaches and psychosocial casework, the last being absent from the training of the respondents in the study. Counselling is used but, in common with other theoretical models, it remains a problem for trainees and newly qualified practitioners to unpack how, for what purpose and when specific approaches are relevant. Experienced practitioners still struggle with this issue, although successful or failing practice outcomes begin to define what works. Many social workers, once qualified, seek further counselling and psychotherapeutic training, often at personal expense, to enhance their work and skills. The need for high-quality interpersonal skills is specified in the requirements for post-qualifying awards in social work.

Social workers regularly write in professional journals arguing for the acknowledgement of the need to give more time and attention to these areas of practice, which they feel are becoming marginalized in the current contracting culture. For example, Gwen Bird writes:

> If social workers are to be deeply interested in the quality and character of people's perceptions of their close relationships, as David Howe and Diana Hinnings say (Recovering the Relationship, 31 July–6 August), then social work training might well have something to learn from the training which psycho-dynamic counsellors undergo.
>
> Real understanding and empathy for human suffering and misery caused by relationship difficulties is born out of a professional training which includes two fundamental elements.
>
> First, an in depth study of the theory which underpins early psychological, emotional and social development, such as the work of Donald Winnicott, John Bowlby and Melanie Klein for example, together with the study of more modern writers such as Michael Jacobs and Anthony Storr.
>
> Second, comprehensive self-awareness training that enables a practitioner to work from a position of strong inner stability, and not as Howe and Hinnings point out, cause them to be 'phased by the emotional ups and downs of difficult cases' or 'react defensively'.
>
> Combining these two major elements in my own training with experiential work has enabled me to work with a feeling of confidence which is the result of understanding each client in a holistic way.
>
> (Bird 1997: 15)

This book argues that for all social work tasks it is important to have at least basic counselling skills, and preferably to have more advanced ones, even if it is not necessary for all social workers to be qualified to counsel in depth. What is required depends upon the setting in which the workers are employed.

These basic skills can be identified as:

- attention giving, active listening, non-critical acceptance;
- paraphrasing, reflecting back, summarizing and checking;

- awareness of the use of different kinds of questions, minimal prompting, use of alternatives to questions;
- empathic understanding, linking, immediacy;
- challenging, confronting, work with defences;
- goal setting, problem solving, focusing techniques;
- knowledge about own and other's use of body language;
- avoidance of judging and moralistic responses;
- boundary awareness, structuring techniques, the ability to say difficult things constructively;
- the ability to offer feedback, techniques for defusing, avoiding the creation of and managing hostility.

These kinds of skills are well documented in literature across a range of approaches to counselling and interviewing (Nelson-Jones 1981; Jacobs 1982; Egan 1990). They are essential to the counselling process and also to facilitating tasks such as benefits advice, community care assessments, pre-sentence report interviews, assessment of children and support plans. They can be used in case management across client groups and in many other core social work functions at the office, in care establishments and in people's own homes.

The theoretical models best known to social workers to underpin skills are those of Carl Rogers and the psychodyamic theories. Both models offer ideas about the personality which influence the way in which the worker may relate to the person they are helping. A familiar framework to many social workers, which matches many social work tasks well, is the one outlined by Gerard Egan and cited by Francesca Inskipp (1986: 18) in summary form as follows.

Inskipp describes how in *Stage 1* the helper develops a warm relationship which enables the client to explore 'the problem' from his or her own frame of reference. Together the worker and client move on to focus on specific concerns. The skills associated with this phase are:

1 Attention giving.
2 Listening.
3 Active listening:
  - communicating, empathic understanding;
  - non-critical acceptance;
  - genuineness;

by
- paraphrasing;
- reflecting feelings;
- summarizing;
- focusing, helping the client to be specific;
- paraphrasing, reflecting feelings, summarizing.

Stage 2 is concerned with developing new understandings. Clients are helped to see themselves and their situations in a new perspective. The worker and client focus on what might help the client to cope more effectively. They consider what strengths and resources the client might use. The skills used are all the skills of Stage 1, plus:

1 Communicating deeper empathic understanding and hunches, 'hearing the music behind the words'.
2 Helping the client to recognize themes, inconsistencies.
3 Giving information.
4 Sharing the helper's feelings and/or experiences.
5 'You–me talk' – what is happening between us (immediacy).
6 Goal setting.

Stage 3 is where the client is helped to consider possible ways to act, to look at costs and consequences, to plan action, implement it and evaluate it. This is a goal setting phase and uses all the skills of Stages 1 and 2, plus:

1 Creative thinking and brainstorming.
2 Problem solving and decision making.
3 Using learning theory to plan action.
4 Evaluating.

Since this summary was written, Egan has made *evaluation* a fourth stage, in which the client and worker evaluate outcomes and appraise any changes needed together.

This formulation of counselling skills into a progressive action framework is a useful one for beginning social workers. It also probably provides a sufficient range of skills, if taught in detail in practice sessions, to equip practitioners for most social work interviews, with clear 'stop off' points, depending on the task or level of intervention. Most social workers find themselves undertaking some supportive counselling in the course of their work, for which this may be sufficient. Those social workers who work in agencies such as post-adoption, fertility or other specialized counselling require more specific knowledge and skills.

While planning this book, I attempted to verify whether these skills are being used as I thought, through a small survey of social workers. These were practitioners who had completed a university-based counselling course and were still practising in social work. It showed them to be using counselling skills regularly. Those selected for the survey had participated and completed counselling studies work to merit level or above over three years. They were also practising social workers in a range of settings, including mental health, general hospital, children and families teams, adult services, group care and fieldwork. The questionnaire was therefore sent only to people who had clearly demonstrated knowledge of counselling skills practice alongside social work practice. Twenty-five out of thirty responded, showing the outcome in Table 1.1.

Respondents were asked to indicate the use in their daily social work practice of the skills listed. All the figures are percentages of the total of returned questionnaires. The outcome for this sample shows listening skills to be the most used and confronting the least, although every skill is used to a considerable extent. It was impossible without follow-up interviews to make inferences about the comparative use of skills or the use of skills for specific purposes from such a small sample. However, the survey confirms that qualified and competent practitioners in both counselling and social work consistently use counselling skills to underpin and carry out their day-by-day social work roles and tasks.

This book focuses on skills for practice. However, it is important to reflect that in the area of interpersonal skills, technical proficiency alone is not enough. The attitudes and style of the worker are also important in achieving good outcomes. This was asserted by Truax and Carkhuff (1967: 141): 'Research seems consistently to find empathy, warmth, genuineness characteristic of human encounters that change people for the better.' This use of the self in relationship as the prerequisite for changing the other is strongly restated in the person-centred and the psychodynamic approaches to counselling, where the conditions for

Table 1.1 Use of counselling skills in daily practice by social workers

	Percentage using skill			
Skill	*Always*	*Often*	*Sometimes*	*Never*
Attention giving	71	29	0	0
Listening	93	7	0	0
Active listening	57	43	0	0
Use of empathy	28	64	8	0
Acceptance	57	28	15	0
Genuineness	28	57	15	0
Paraphrasing	30	35	35	0
Reflecting back	30	34	36	0
Summarizing	38	38	24	0
Questions/explore	20	60	20	0
Minimal prompts	21	54	25	0
Challenging	7	43	50	0
Confronting	0	56	44	0
Linking	7	50	43	0
Immediacy	7	53	40	0
Work on defences	7	40	53	0
Goal setting	28	36	36	0
Problem solving	36	64	0	0

therapeutic relationships are explored in detail (Jacobs 1982; Mearns and Thorne 1988).

What appears to make the difference between effective and ineffective therapists is the degree of warmth and respect towards individuals which Carl Rogers (1961) formulated as being among the core conditions for person-centred practice. These are described by person-centred practitioners as congruence, advanced accurate empathy and unconditional positive regard. These core conditions have equally always underpinned analytic/psychodynamic therapy and social casework, even if they are sometimes more readily assumed in the literature.

Whatever counselling theory is used, it is the personal relationship and facilitating qualities of the worker that are valued, as much as skills and theoretical models, by recipients of services. This has been known and accepted ever since the research completed by Truax and Carkhuff. There has been no contrary evidence to invalidate this finding. Current research into social work delivery finds contemporary evidence to similar effect. For example, Hardiker and Barker (1994) found social workers relying on casework and counselling skills to facilitate complex work in cases of significant harm under the Children Act 1989. Aldgate and Bradley (1999) found that the clients valued the personal support, as it was viewed, of the social workers who planned respite as much as they appreciated the service provided.

In many social work settings more advanced skills can considerably enhance worker performance and confidence. Areas to consider here are work with bereaved people, interviews with abused young people, work with people suffering from depression or other mental health difficulties, work with substance users or offenders. The narrative examples of practitioners' work that appear later in this book show the varied use of beginning and advanced skills in everyday social work practice.

Social workers and counsellors all work towards helping individuals to change, adjust to a change in life circumstances or find new opportunities and resources to grow and develop. The key difference, perhaps, is that while people come for counselling almost entirely of their own free will, those using social work services are often compelled by societal or legal mandates to address a particular area of their lives, or are driven to ask for help by poverty or some other type of disadvantage. The dimension that clearly differentiates counselling from social work is therefore context. Counsellors do not have to engage with service delivery or directly with their clients' social environments. They can offer confidentiality in a distinctive way, and can operate in neatly contracted hourly sessions within discrete agencies.

This means that counselling can be defined by the British Association for Counselling (BAC) as:

> People become engaged in counselling when a person occupying regularly or temporarily the role of counsellor offers or agrees explicitly to offer time, attention and respect to another person or persons, temporarily in the role of client.

> The task of counselling is to give the client an opportunity to explore, discover and clarify ways of living more resourcefully and toward greater well-being.

This definition might also apply to some parts of a social worker's contract with a service user, but social workers exercise their counselling skills in legal, procedural and resourcing frameworks. These acutely affect the boundaries and responsibilities that they have and the ways in which counselling skills may be exercised. These other goals and aims would make BAC's definition insufficient as a working agreement. Examples of such goal-directed work are: programmes to address offending behaviour, completing community care assessments, helping parents struggling with behavioural issues with children, supporting young people leaving care, undertaking a section 47 enquiry as required by the 1989 Children Act. In these contexts social workers cannot offer complete confidentiality to individuals, because information is often shared between agencies; nor can they ensure what involvement will be needed without considering environmental and legal factors.

Paradoxically, the societal constraints that lead people to become users of social work services, and the compulsory nature of some of the work, means that social workers are often working with some of the most distressed, disadvantaged and troubled people in the community; people who might benefit from an in-depth counselling approach. Likewise, teams of social workers find themselves suddenly involved in post-disaster counselling (e.g. Lockerbie, Dunblane) or situations which demand intensive input when emotions are running high. This means a need for interpersonal skills of the highest order. This was recognized in the lobby for a three-year training for social work, and is now being recognized in the modules being developed for post-qualifying training. The complexity of skills, knowledge and values needed for social work practice makes the current two-year initial training a sound enough base (Marsh and Triseliotis 1996b). However, two years is not a long time for integrating what is learned, and certainly not for developing advanced levels of interpersonal skills. Many practising social workers identify the need for further training. Certainly the basic counselling skills, once acquired, are quickly put into practice.

One new intake worker describes this:

> I remember on my first day as a new intake worker I interviewed: first, a very abusive large man who needed furniture

for a new flat and whose anger with a benefits refusal was being directed at me; second, a woman living alone with four young children whose electricity was about to be disconnected and who in contrast was weepy, distracted and desperate; third, a terrified and shocked young couple who had just been subjected to a terrible experience of racist abuse, in which their flat had been vandalized and covered in graffiti because she was a young black person living with a white man; fourth, an elderly man who seemed confused about why he had come and who finally told me he had ants in the kitchen and didn't know how to get rid of them. That was only the morning!

All those people needed practical assistance and also, in different ways, wanted understanding related to the way they were feeling. They wanted time to talk as well as practical assistance or information as to where to obtain resources or what action to take next. They all were helped by the use of counselling skills in facilitating the interview but none wanted counselling as such.

Also, as Coulshed (1991: 44) writes, 'If case management is to succeed as a strategy for organising and coordinating services at the level of the individual client it has to concentrate on the minutiae of interactions between helper and helped. In this, counselling plays a pivotal role.'

Summary

Practical counselling skills are relevant to social work practice at all levels and in all settings. This is because:

- Relationships remain at the heart of effective practice.
- The basic ethic of respect for others underpins both counselling and social work as disciplines and is crucial to culturally sensitive practice. Social work should be based on non-stigmatizing process facilitated by good interpersonal skills.
- Work across the life cycle involves social workers in crisis intervention and other counselling roles.
- Practitioners evidence the usefulness of counselling skills.

• The outcomes of research into effective practice repeatedly give the message that users value this kind of approach.

I return to these key themes in the final chapter, but they re-emerge from time to time throughout.

In the following chapters, I consider the ways in which counselling skills are needed to underpin everyday social work. I consider this by looking in turn at each of the six core competences which trainee social workers are expected to achieve in work-based practice placements when studying for the Diploma in Social Work, and which they are expected to demonstrate throughout their subsequent professional practice. These competences will be familiar to social workers who qualified from 1997 onwards, or those who have been teaching student social workers, but perhaps not to others. For those who did not qualify recently, it is important to say that these categories reflect developments in the history of social work theory and practice. Although I shall be considering ideas which are expressed in the new language of competence, I believe they will be easily recognized by any social worker as integral to good practice.

Even as I write, discussion is under way to reappraise the role of CCETSW in training and to consider the possibility of setting up a Social Care Council. Whatever the outcome of current debates, it is possible that social work training will face more change as the agenda of populations and politicians shifts. However, I remain confident that whether practice learning curricula change or not, in some form or other these six areas of practice activity remain important components in which all social carers, at whatever level, should show ability in order to obtain a recognized qualification. They are:

• communicate and engage;
• promote and enable;
• assess and plan;
• intervene and provide services;
• work in organizations;
• develop professional competence (CCETSW 1995).

Each chapter therefore considers the social work theory and method which may be involved in meeting each requirement and gives some history of its inclusion as a core competence for social work. Some practice narratives are included in each chapter, showing how the use of counselling skills (not extended therapeutic counselling) is embedded in and underpins the work, focusing throughout on the links between values, knowledge and skills as they are enmeshed in the fabric of the helping process.

Chapter 2

To communicate and engage: relevant counselling skills

Communication in social work is a two-way process, with the aim of engaging the service user with the worker in a plan of action to achieve a specified goal. CCETSW chose in 1995 to make this the foundation competence for qualifying social workers who have to demonstrate that they can:

> Communicate and engage within communities to promote opportunities for service users at risk or in need to function, participate and develop in society.
>
> (CCETSW 1995)

This decision:

- reflects the history in social work of preoccupation with listening, responding and interpersonal skills as a foundation for social work processes;
- acknowledges the need for trainee social workers to develop sound interpersonal skills in relating to the public and other professionals.

The skills needed to underpin these human interactions are derived from the practice of social casework (Richmond 1922; Perlman 1957; Hollis 1964), and they have subsequently been developed by Compton and Galaway (1989) and Coulshed (1991).

Social casework has its origins in psychoanalysis and the associated literature that has permeated the helping professions, including medicine, counselling, education and pastoral care. From these a core of listening, attending and counselling skills are derived, useful in a range of communication and relationship tasks. This chapter considers the part that counselling skills play in the achievement of this competence in social work.

Communication in social work practice involves more than imparting information. It is a process where thoughts, feelings, ideas and hopes are not only exchanged between people, but also need to be understood together. Verbal and non-verbal communications are used to:

- transmit and share information;
- establish relationship;
- exchange ideas and perceptions;
- create change;
- exchange attitudes, values and beliefs;
- achieve worker and user goals.

It is important that in this exchange workers respect the values and beliefs of others as far as is consistent with their professional authority and function. Meanings must be carefully checked, and in each exchange, care needs to be taken to be aware of, and reduce, the blocks to communication that can come from the many differences between individuals, such as authority and power, language, ability and disability, personality, background, gender, health, age, race, class. Other barriers may impede communication, such as environment, the pressure of limited available time, the involvement of other people, the physical environment or interruptions. Genuine communication is only achieved if the barriers are considered and worked through or removed.

Lago and Thompson (1996: 40), writing about cultural barriers to communication in counselling, suggest a similar range of possible dimensions:

> language, time, context, purpose of meeting, views and attitudes towards each other, location of meeting, customs/ rituals, smell, age, touch, disability, decoration, adornment, jewelry, personal institutional power, expectations,

perceptions of previous personal history, context of meeting, why they are meeting, conventions of greeting and meeting behaviour, gender, notions of acceptable/unacceptable behaviour, system of ethics/morals, interpersonal projections, political differences, personal theories of communication, physical appearance, height, weight, non verbal behaviour.

Each meeting between two human beings, carrying their own cultural conditionings, can be seen to have several dimensions of difference and assumptions as well as similarities. Lago and Thompson (1996: 41) suggest that the 'counsellor may have considerable difficulty in fully offering one of the core therapeutic conditions as defined by Rogers (1961) for successful therapy to occur, that of acceptance or non-judgementalism.' They also usefully remind the reader that awareness of cultural dimensions of counselling should not be used to conceal prejudice or racism within the counsellor.

These dimensions of difference can also be barriers in social work practice. The addition of social work power through role and law adds a very particular dimension to the human encounters which take place in a variety of office and home settings. The concern of social workers to avoid discrimination in carrying out their roles and duties makes it especially important to diminish communication barriers as far as possible. However, this has to be balanced with awareness of role and function, as well as caution about concealed or unacknowledged power on the part of the worker. For example:

• Social workers are daily working with people who are made vulnerable because of age or disability (abused children, confused older people, the mentally ill) or through circumstances (denial of rights, eviction, bereavement). This makes it important not to use communication skills to cajole, manipulate or persuade someone into a course of action which he or she may not really want or to pacify someone whose rights are being negated. At the same time, if a social worker's duty to society or someone else's safety (e.g. a child's) means that difficult things have to be said, skills are needed to communicate this honestly, so that the real meanings and consequences of legally mandated actions are understood. The possibility of the misuse of delegated power through verbal abilities is an ethical consideration of the utmost importance.

- Sometimes users of social work services are voluntary, but frequently they are not. The element of compulsion or social control in practice means that social workers cannot, as counsellors can, choose only to work with people who are motivated towards the process in which they are engaged. This adds barriers of reluctance, hostility and resistance to many encounters. The ability to communicate and establish relationship, to establish purpose and to engage people in effective working in these circumstances needs acutely developed and refined skills, especially as anxiety and anger are likely to be very much in evidence.

- Social workers need to develop skills in communicating with a range of users whose ability for verbal communication is either reduced or not fully developed. This includes older people with dementia, adults with learning disabilities and adults with a range of impairments such as hearing loss. Social workers need to be able to communicate effectively with young children. Learning to interview children therapeutically, and when required to establish video evidence for a court hearing, is an advanced skill. Social workers also need abilities in using Makaton or other facilitated communication methods, and at the very least need to know how best to ensure that communication is two-way (e.g. interpreting services of various kinds).

Communication can be viewed as an interactive process involving the giving, receiving and checking out of meaning. Communication occurs on many levels and may not always be congruent. Role relationships are an important dimension and barriers to communication should be considered. It is crucial that interviewers tune into the potential barriers created by differences such as age, class or ethnicity. Communication is a process of which the outcome is engagement, the beginning of a further process where the parties are able to work together, to be involved, to achieve mutual understanding, to hold attention and to contract to a purpose.

Communication skills have been the bedrock of social work practice, and other professions need abilities in communicating. For example, medicine is finding that the failure of doctors to communicate well is at the root of many complaints (Moore 1997; Smith and Norton 1999). Consequently, more attention has been paid to communication skills in doctor and nurse training. Social workers in hospitals frequently find themselves using their own counselling skills in communication to clarify miscommunication and the subsequent lack of engagement. Social workers aim for the active involvement of people, so that they can be empowered to change their own situations or have more control and knowledge within them.

Practice example
The following narrative shows how a block in communication, which was producing conflict between a patient and his doctor, was resolved through the use of counselling skills by a hospital social worker.

Mr Mistry was a hospital patient being cared for on a medical ward. He was a black man born in India, and his first language was Gujerati. The social worker was a white woman, born in Britain, whose first language was English. The doctor was a white man, born in Britain, but of Eastern European ancestry. His first language was English.

The service user was in hospital after experiencing a stroke. He had completed his drug therapy and was described as medically stable by the doctor. He was referred to the social work team, because he was reluctant to comply with further treatment, which included physiotherapy and occupational therapy. He had refused to go to the gym for exercise. The doctor described the patient as having become 'lazy' and adopting the 'classic sick role'. Exploration of this with the doctor brought out that he thought that the patient enjoyed the sick role and liked the idea of people doing everything for him, including dressing and feeding him. The conclusion from this was that the service user would be best placed in a nursing home, where he could remain dependent and be looked after by other people.

The social worker's first step was to visit the service user, but with an interpreter to check that the communication between the user and worker was accurate. The service user clearly stated that he did not want to go into a nursing home, and that he wanted to go home. He knew that as he lived alone he would need to be able to wash, dress and feed himself in order to be safe. In this interview he did not appear to be enjoying the sick role and seemed to want to return home as soon as possible (skills used here: *active listening, attending, listening to body language, use of interpreting service, checking, so enabling worker and patient to communicate, empathy*).

At the end of this first interview there was a contradiction between what the service user was saying and the original referral information. At the next meeting, the worker shared with the service user her puzzlement over what was happening (*immediacy*). She asked why, if he was wanting to get better, he didn't comply with the treatment (*exploratory open-ended question*). He replied that he had complied, as he had taken all of his tablets. The worker then understood from Mr Mistry that he saw medicine as treatment. He thought that the doctor no longer believed that he had been ill and was sending him to the gym for exercise to prove that he was no longer ill. Since then there had been a block in communication and understanding between Mr Mistry and the ward and he had not been enabled to participate in the follow-up treatment.

The social worker had established that there was miscommunication and now decided to observe the interaction between the doctor and the patient. She reflected on the use of language between the two people. Her conclusion was that both the medical stance and the language used were moralistic, judgemental and authoritarian. The client was judged as lazy, a decision about him that had been made quickly, without checking, and in an authoritarian mode of knowing best. The worker considered that the medical model of communication was often from a controlling parent ego-state (*ego psychology/transactional analysis theoretical model*). This was possibly arousing resistance (*a defence*) in the service user. As she reflected upon Mr Mistry's language, he was using phrases like 'I will not. He cannot make me', reflecting the kind of responses which can come from the dependency of childhood, and which may be aroused in adults through illness and helplessness. The anger and resistance that can accompany such feelings where there is a parental attitude in the helper reinforce the difficulties of dependency (*child ego-state*).

The worker recognized that neither of the two parties was being helpful to the other, and that they were instead reinforcing polarized attitudes. The more the doctor acted as a controlling parent, the more the service user refused to work as he was prescribed. This analysis enabled the worker to focus clearly on the way in which the doctor and patient were reinforcing their miscommunication.

The worker suggested a meeting between the doctor and Mr Mistry, with herself present. She invited the doctor to explain to the service user the treatment benefits being suggested, in that it would build up his muscles, improve his ability to walk and enable him to gain strength before being at home alone. She asked Mr Mistry to explain that he had refused the treatment because he had thought that he needed to be really fit to use a gym, and that rest was the best cure. He had thought that the doctor regarded him as fit. (Here the worker used her empathy for the views of both people to set up a meeting to clarify and summarize the actual intentions of both people, using counselling skills in mediation as she challenged the authority model constructively.) At this meeting, the two 'sides' were able to exchange information and perceptions as one adult to another. The service user was able to hear and understand that physiotherapy was offered to increase his possible rehabilitation. The doctor began to understand that the service user was reluctant to use the gym for other reasons, not from laziness or unexplained reluctance (*challenge to perspectives, the enabling of the lowering of defences on the patient's part*).

The worker, by her early involvement of the interpreter, had checked that two-way communication could happen. She reduced the power imbalance between the hospital and the service user, who was able to have his voice heard. By valuing both people equally and by *attentive listening*, she established where the misunderstanding was, and examined the frames of reference of both people carefully. She used her skills (*listening, summarizing, use of questions, empathy*) to facilitate a meeting to work out a solution. She did this by her *immediacy* and understanding to facilitate a three-way conversation that unblocked the impasse and enabled Mr Mistry to receive the services to which he was entitled in dignified and adult mode.

The worker's analysis of her actions demonstrated her knowledge, values and skills. She explored the cultural context in which she was working and considered how far her theoretical model was applicable. There was a clear cultural difference between the doctor's belief that the patient would improve with active rehabilitation and the patient's belief that he should rest and pass the time quietly to improve. There were power differentials created by role and status. Her role was to remain non-judgemental and objective, while acknowledging boundaries that both supported the client and provided a service for the hospital. The worker discussed the boundaries of her role with the client and doctor, so as to be explicit about their transactions.

Interviewing

Most social work communication takes place through the medium of interviewing, in offices, on the telephone or in the person's home. The social work interview has been described in various ways: for example, Davies (1985) calls it a 'conversation with a purpose', while Hugman (1977) argues for social workers to 'act natural'. Personal attributes such as warmth, flexibility and creativity have been considered a good base from which to begin. However, the majority of social work literature on communication and relationship argues for a combination of warmth, empathy and positive regard with skills which have been developed through supervised practice, whether simulated or actual.

Compton and Galaway (1989: 334) offer a useful synthesis, describing the social work interview as, 'a set of communications with four special characteristics: (1) it has a context or a setting; (2) it is purposeful and directed; (3) it is limited and contractual; (4) it involves specialised role relationships.'

There are many useful books to help students with the theoretical structuring and purposes of this process (Nelson-Jones 1981; Breakwell 1990; Heron 1997; Millar and Rollnick 1991). Social work programmes can teach basic skills and practice placements can test them. The difficult part for trainees is the transfer of learning to practice in the beginning stages, although interviewing techniques remain the subject of a lifetime's practice and development. Research appears to show that interviewing skills can be taught and developed through the practice and rehearsal of microskills (Bamford and Dickson 1995), and can be transferred into the workplace (Ryan *et al.* 1995). The next section considers the core counselling foundation skills and how they are applicable for social workers seeking to communicate and engage.

Core communication skills

Listening

In social work this is an active process, and not just a series of 'nods' and the overuse of 'mms' that might provoke hostility and impatience in the service user. The guidelines offered by Jacobs (1985: 13) are helpful here:

- listen with undivided attention, without interrupting;
- remember what has been said, including the details (the more you listen and the less you say the better your memory);
- listen to the base line (what is not openly said but possibly is being felt);
- watch for non-verbal clues to help you understand the feelings;
- listen to yourself and how you might feel in a described situation, as a way of further understanding (empathy);
- try to tolerate pauses and silences that are a little longer than is usual in conversations, and avoid asking lots of questions to break silences;

- help yourself and the other to feel comfortable and relaxed with each other, keeping calm even when you don't feel calm.

While checklists are helpful in guiding actions, supervised live practice is essential. Many people think when they read such guidelines that this is what they already do, only to be amazed to find in simulated practice that, for example, they find silence less easy to tolerate than they thought, or are not clear how to paraphrase well. The ability to listen and hear and hold in a focused way is essential. Cornwall (1980: 17–18) writes helpfully about listening as part of the context of empowering practice: 'if listening is selective it disallows the other person choice in setting the agenda . . . if listening is open with positive unconditional regard and lack of negative judgement, this offers the gift of space and the discharge of internal pain leading to a sense of control over the self which is empowering.'

It is also useful to identify some of the features of ordinary conversation which are not so helpful in professional interviews. An interesting formulation of these is described by Townsend (1987: 21). They are:

- daydreaming (losing attention, thoughts wandering);
- labelling (putting the other person into a category before hearing the evidence);
- scoring points (relating everything you hear to your own experience);
- mind reading (predicting what the other person is thinking);
- rehearsing (practising your next lines in your head);
- cherrypicking (listening for a key piece of information and then switching off);
- interrupting (being unable to resist giving advice);
- duelling (countering the speaker's verbal advances with parries and thrusts of your own);
- side-stepping sentiment (countering expressions of emotion with jokes or cliches).

Conversely, accurate and good listening in an interview context: tries to understand and hear the experience of the other; keeps an open mind about what may be said next; waits until the other has finished speaking and reflects upon it before responding;

does not select what will be important in advance; keeps focused on the other's agenda; does not label or stereotype; does not advise until advice is requested and a full picture is obtained; does not make provocative or challenging comments thoughtlessly; makes space for the other to express and clarify feeling.

It is possible to imagine the distorted assessment of risk concerning a child, or the inaccurately constructed care plan for an adult which comes from an interview where the social worker has 'cherrypicked' or 'labelled'. It is all the more important that users are heard by social workers because by the time they reach the agency, they are often angry or frustrated by the labelling or hostility they have met elsewhere. There are times when, after listening carefully to the person's story, the social worker cannot offer a service, or needs to make a referral. However, the person who has been thoughtfully heard finds this more acceptable than the person who feels dismissed and 'brushed off'. Listening skills can assist the worker to give a personal and non-bureaucratic response without compromising the agency remit. Difficult information can be heard better in an atmosphere which is kept calm and constructive by the social worker.

Responding

Counselling requires thoughtful and measured responses from the counsellor. Social work equally requires skilled and accurate responses. Initially responses may be non-verbal, but it is crucial to begin to offer more than token monosyllables to indicate that the speaker is being heard. Counselling skills such as summarizing, reflecting and paraphrasing are useful to check that information is correctly understood and recorded and to ensure that the services offered meet the expressed need. Learning to do this accurately takes time and practice. The skills listed by Jacobs (1985) can be used to begin to move an interview forward, to clarify or explore more fully.

- Be as accurate as possible in describing feelings and ideas that you perceived (not just depressed or angry).
- Use your empathic understanding to make this accurate, although tentatively, as you could be wrong.

- Keep questions to a minimum unless you need precise information (in which case ask precise questions), want to open up an area (use open questions), wish to prompt (rhetorical questions help here). Avoid questions beginning with why.
- Use minimal prompts (mm, yes or the last few words).
- Paraphrase, summarize or reflect accurately as a way of prompting, an indication that you have been listening, a way of checking that you have heard accurately.
- Avoid making judgements or loaded remarks.
- Where possible link reported experiences, events, reactions and ideas.
- Avoid changing the subject or interrupting unnecessarily.
- Avoid speaking too soon, too often or for too long.

These basic counselling skills may be employed in social work interviews in order to gather information, to enable the person to communicate his or her needs and concerns, to assess what the agency might offer and to pave the way for action or problem solving.

Questioning

Much social work involves gathering initial information from which to make an assessment and/or to provide a service and/or to take some action. Many interventions arise from a personal crisis in the person's life to which social workers are expected to respond quickly. This makes it all the more important to cultivate sound interviewing and interpersonal skills. Some of the forms which social workers need to complete with people are long and time-consuming. Interviews therefore need to be shaped to elicit necessary information as efficiently as possible. In these circumstances, honesty about the need to ask a series of questions is facilitative, since obtaining the information otherwise is too time-consuming. Some areas of work, such as benefits advice, require detailed questioning and information collection. Explanation of the purposes and outcomes of given information (e.g. who will see it or with whom it may be shared) is very important.

Social workers inevitably have to talk more and be more active in their interviews than most counsellors. In order to remember detailed information social workers often make notes and fill forms out in the presence of clients. Explicit reference to this process and obtaining cooperation in checking and agreeing detail is valuable. Counselling skills such as the use of paraphrase, summary and immediacy can be employed. It facilitates an interview if strings of interrogatory and intrusive questions are avoided. Questions which are phrased carefully or alternatives to questions may be used to obtain information. For example, the interviewer can say 'Could you tell me about' or 'It would be helpful to know more about', instead of firing blunt questions to obtain information.

It is essential to be able to distinguish between closed and open questions. Closed ones are needed to elicit specific information, but even a question like 'Are you on medication?' flows better when rephrased as 'Can you tell me what medication you are currently taking?' This may be a closed question but it is less interrogatory in its phrasing. Interviewers who use open questions find the interview progresses better if these can begin with 'how', 'what' or 'when', rather than 'why'. The question 'Why . . . ?' can sound both accusing and overly authoritarian, with echoes of schooldays and childhood. (Why are you late? Why didn't you wash up?) This is particularly important to remember when working with children and young people in adolescence. People are often unsure of the direct reasons for their actions. They can answer a question like 'Why' more easily if a less direct invitation to speak like 'Tell me about the day when the incident happened' is used to enable them to explore motivations.

These techniques centre on careful use of language and phrasing. They still promote explicit interviewing, but phrase questions in ways that can reduce hostility and anxiety. Judgements, loaded remarks and expressions of moralizing are to be avoided because they create defensiveness. Social workers do not confront people with aspects of themselves such as offending or maltreating children in a way that is clumsy or unplanned, either of which may be counterproductive. Personal disapproval or dislike of the service user is something to be taken to supervision, not to be openly expressed to the client. The use of open interviewing is essential in situations where evidence for a court or information for a meeting such as a case conference is needed. Particular care needs to be taken not to ask leading questions or put words into the mouths of service users.

Body language

While cultural diversity about what is and is not acceptable in terms of eye contact, touch, dress and so on needs to be considered at all times, there are some basic areas to keep in mind. For example, it is usually best to ensure that a comfortable distance is observed between the interviewer and client. Arrange not to be interrupted unnecessarily. Consider the informality or formality of the room. Looking distracted, yawning, peering at your watch etc. give clear negative messages. Facial expression is important, since frowns or smiles at inappropriate moments give the wrong message. The lower tones of the voice generally carry better and are calming. Speaking quietly and very clearly to small children is more effective than saying too much, too fast, in a shrill tone. These guidelines from counselling literature are all useful when transferred across to social work settings. Assertiveness, attention to body posture, facial expressions, breathing and seating are all factors that can facilitate the environment and decrease anger, hostility, anxiety or tension. Interviewing in other people's homes means negotiating distractions like radios, TVs, pets and neighbours. Social workers need to take care that the climate is right for an effective interview and must be prepared to address distractions in an assertive but sensitive way.

Practice example

The following account shows how beginning skills were exercised in a criminal justice setting. An initial relationship with the client had to be built and the worker had to communicate and engage to establish a base for future cooperative work.

Dean was a young adult male with a wife and baby who was referred from a magistrates court subject to a six-month probation order made for drinking and driving. This was a second offence. The major objectives facing the officer were to *confront* the offender with the impact of this offence on his family and the community, and to look at the risks he was taking. He had to be seen weekly. At the first interview the major task was to *check out* that Dean understood what was expected of him in terms of attendance at meetings and participation in the programme. He was offered the opportunity to give his own thoughts and reactions to events. A joint plan of action was created.

The outcome was a client who could articulate and accept the dangers of drink driving and acknowledge the need to control his alcohol intake for the sake of his wife and child and the community. He did not re-offend during the order. He dealt with some practical issues around housing and employment which had been causing anxiety and therefore drinking. He attended a group for motoring offenders. The worker, as is usual in social work, employed a variety of approaches: individual work, group process and practical assistance. All these were based on communication and the building of a relationship to engage the client.

First, information was given carefully, to show a clear understanding of process (*checking, paraphrasing, summarizing*). The client was asked to give his perspective on his situation (*use of empathy*). He was encouraged to identify his own strengths (*ego support*) and say where he needed help (*linking, problem solving, goal setting*). His initial playing down of the offence was discussed and reframed (*challenge*). The worker treated Dean as an individual (*genuineness, acceptance*) and valued him as a person, while not minimizing the drinking and driving (*attentive listening*). To explore the potential causes and effects of the offence, *open questions* were used. At the beginning of the work the worker endeavoured to put Dean at ease and tried to give *body messages* of *attentiveness* and *active listening*. The court had already passed sentence, so moralistic and judging responses could be avoided. The practitioner said: 'I reflected back his own feelings and behaviour. I was aware of the need to challenge where appropriate and motivate Dean into accepting responsibility and recognizing the impact that this offence caused his victims.'

Whatever the long-term outcome, in the short term thorough purposeful and boundaried interactions, based on carefully chosen techniques and skills, enabled the worker to meet agency objectives. Dean gained verbal and cognitive awareness of himself and his behaviour.

Skills in communication and engagement are crucial to sustaining a working social work relationship from the initial contact onwards. Careful listening, observing and responding to oneself and the other enables exchanges of meaning which make the work effective. The use of such skills is particularly important in clarifying expectations and challenging and maintaining the authority role given by the court, while seeking to work to a client's strengths and own goals for his or her life.

Frameworks for interviewing

Counsellors in most settings are able to offer hourly sessions for a specific length of time in which to address particular issues identified as troublesome by the client. Social workers are usually employed to work within clear legal or agency mandates. The role usually expects that practical problem solving is undertaken. The matters which users bring are as frequently defined by other people as by themselves. Issues of risk to the self or public feature highly. The accountability with which the social worker is invested on behalf of society is very important, and society's investment in this is sometimes demonstrated vigorously, when things go wrong, in the media and through public inquiries. This accountability has led social workers to organize their interviewing into frameworks which help to achieve the agency's and user's identified goals.

The following frameworks have been widely used to facilitate communication and engagement. A brief summary is offered here which can be followed up, using the references provided.

- *Solution-focused therapy*. This approach derives from the work of de Shazer (1985, 1988). The worker's focus is on enabling people to identify their own established solutions to difficulties and supporting them to sustain change. The emphasis is less on problems and more on reinforcing coping strategies which have already succeeded for the client.
- *Motivational interviewing*. This approach is described by Millar and Rollnick (1991). It is essentially a practical eclectic approach, with workers assisting clients to recognize and build on their own abilities to change. Five principles for intervention are

described in detail: express empathy, develop discrepancy, avoid argumentation, roll with resistance, support self-efficacy.

- *Humanistic frameworks.* Heron (1997) presents six intervention styles for face-to-face helping. These are prescriptive, informative, confronting, cathartic, catalytic, supportive. These detailed responses are related to choices about intervention made by therapists and clients together to meet need. The approach clarifies for practitioners which kinds of intervention are most useful in which situation.
- *Cognitive frameworks.* Cognitive approaches are effective in both social work and psychotherapeutic interventions. Examples can be found in the work of Roberts (1995), Ryle (1995) and Corey (1997). In recent years research has shown the effectiveness of such approaches in working with offenders and other specific groups of people (McGuire 1995).

Counselling skills are described to underpin all these different frameworks for interviewing and engaging the client. I shall consider the way counselling skills can underpin different theoretical approaches and problem solving frameworks for social work further in Chapter 5.

> *Practice example*
> This chapter concludes with a further example that shows how a social worker may use counselling skills to communicate and engage with a family in work within the legal framework of the requirements under the Children Act 1989 to safeguard the welfare of a child.
> The stepfather and birth mother of a young child had applied to adopt him formally, giving the stepfather full parental responsibility, together with the child's birth mother. The formal role of the local authority in such proceedings is to assess whether the granting of such an application is in the child's best interest. The local authority also has a duty between the application and the hearing date to: make inquiries and be satisfied as to the welfare of the child; advise the prospective adopters about the full legal implications of such an order, and its effects on them and the child; advise on alternative courses of action. A written report gives information to the court

about the family, their circumstances, the likely outcome of the proposed adoption, the child's welfare and any alternative action that might be better for the child. Part of the social worker's responsibility is to ascertain the feelings and wishes of children and to ensure that they are informed of changes that affect them. They therefore also need skills in communicating with children.

In this narrative the child was very young (six years old) and the family were finding it difficult to tell him about his origins and why the mother and 'father' were applying to a court to adopt him. The worker knew from research and practice that making the child clear about his identity and origins was the best policy in this situation. She shared this information with the adults and offered to work with them to make sure their son was aware of his life circumstances, including the proposed adoption.

Initially she used *empathy* to think what the process might be like for the family. She worked with the parents to construct a story book which in picture and simple word form could be read to the little boy. It was designed as an ongoing project, so that he had his storybook with all the important events chronicled, on which he could build later. With the adults the social worker allowed space in her communications (*use of silence*), which meant the family could think and reflect and respond. She used *open-ended questions* when exploring their domestic arrangements and parenting roles and capabilities, in order to avoid being oppressive. She involved everyone in discussions so that communication in the family stayed open. With the child, she played, read and drew, at all times trying to use simple, clear language without jargon. Thus she was able to discuss, *listen, empathize* and *counsel* through their different concerns. Families in this situation are often surprised by unanticipated social work attention, and resistant.

These adults were anxious about telling the child that he was born to the mother prior to the marriage, and the circumstances of his father. However, sensitive use of personal skills, combined with honesty about process and judicious use of power, meant that the family were able to become engaged in the process, and gained through it. The worker's counselling skills were a valuable tool in enabling her to put into operation the values of empowerment on which she based her practice. She was thus able to communicate and engage. At each stage, she considered what she needed to achieve and what skills would best achieve the outcome. She used authority in a skilled way to ensure that the child and his family were able to cooperate with her in achieving what the family wanted, in a way that met the child's assessed need to know about his early history.

Conclusion

This chapter shows how counselling skills for the competence to communicate and engage are the foundation for building relationships which engage people in a social work process that is often imposed upon them rather than chosen. They may appear simple skills, but of course they need not only to be learned, but also to be practised in training, in order to develop their use in actual situations. As one student wrote while reflecting on practice:

> combining a practical and realistic approach to theory and employing sound, taught interviewing techniques is the most competent and skilful approach . . . it seems the more practice you get, the more confident you become, and with this your confidence grows, so you become an effective and skilful helper.
>
> (Smith 1994: 12)

Chapter 3

To promote and enable: relevant counselling skills

A primary theme in contemporary social work practice is the focus on facilitating service users' coping mechanisms and strengths to solve difficulties. This contrasts with some notions of 'helping', which are framed in ways that make people unnecessarily dependent or passive. Social workers seek to understand and analyse the ways in which structural barriers reduce the participation of people in society. They endeavour to work in the least stigmatizing and most enabling way available. This approach is found in three main strands of social work literature: the strengths perspective, empowerment and advocacy. Qualifying social workers are expected to show that they can:

> Promote opportunities for people to use their own strengths and expertise to enable them to meet their responsibilities, secure rights and achieve change.
>
> (CCETSW 1995)

This means helping people forward in their lives and encouraging them actively to reach their potential, or a desired outcome, through having the means or authority to do so. This requirement reflects ideologies of identifying and working with users' strengths and of enabling them to meet their own identified goals and objectives and secure their rights. This chapter considers the place in practice of the strengths perspective, empowerment and advocacy, and gives some examples of work where these aims are approached and underpinned by counselling skills.

The strengths approach

This approach is most coherently formulated by Saleeby. In a seminal book, *The Strengths Perspective in Social Work*, Saleeby writes:

> The strengths perspective is not a theory – although developments in that direction become bolder (Rapp 1996). It is a way of thinking about what you do and with whom you do it. It provides a distinctive lens for examining the world of practice. Any approach to practice, in the end, is based on interpretation of the experiences of practitioners and clients and is composed of assumptions, rhetoric, ethics and a set of methods. The importance and usefulness of any practice orientation lies not in some independent measure of truth, but in how well it serves us in our work with people, how it fortifies our values, and how it generates opportunities for clients in a particular environment to change in the direction of their hopes and aspirations.
>
> (Saleeby 1997: 17)

The strengths perspective, when applied in any social work setting, is one which takes an ecological systems approach to problem solving, considering social, political and cultural, as well as individual, accounts of human predicaments and possibilities, focusing not on deficits but on the resourcefulness of the client.

The principles of the approach as presented by Saleeby (1997) are:

• respecting client strengths;
• acknowledging that clients have many strengths;
• client motivation is based on fostering strengths;
• the social worker is a collaborator with the client;
• the victim mind-set is to be avoided;
• any environment is full of resources.

Worker philosophies that follow are:

- empowerment;
- membership/inclusion;
- regeneration;
- synergy;
- dialogue;
- suspension of disbelief.

This approach fits well not only with empowerment philosophies but also with a person-centred approach to the client, as described by Rogers (1961). Counselling skills can be employed in working with people to identify these strengths and promote opportunities for development.

Practice example

The following narrative, provided by a social worker, reflects the way she attempted to integrate the Rogerian concepts of 'genuineness' and 'worth' in a person-centred and strength building way in practice.

The worker reported:

> *genuineness* to be an attitude of mind, achieved as the counsellor grows in confidence and personal maturity, through training and experience. Inherent in this is the idea of *acceptance* and non-judgementalism. This is experienced by the client as *unconditional positive regard*. This communicates to the client a feeling of self-worth which hopefully will facilitate a process of self-acceptance and growth. This does not mean the client's every behaviour is accepted.

The worker then considered the ways in which this style of working could be applied to childcare practice. She suggested that many of the people she met in childcare work were experiencing low self-esteem, often because of difficulties in their parenting of their children. Sometimes this was the outcome of the inadequate parenting that they themselves had experienced. Appreciating this, however, is not the whole story in social work, because, as she said:

The social worker has many roles to play in the job. More and more she has to be an instrument of government and of the legal system, in other words attempting to enforce solutions according to pre-stated procedures. There is still an advisory and advocacy role, and she is also involved in practical work for her clients. Thus she is forced at times to be both 'with' her client and 'against him'.

Thus a person-centred approach to the client is complex, as, for example, people may come to the attention of social workers because of hitting, injuring or neglecting their children. These clients are 'reluctant' or defensive in their interactions with workers. However, it is still possible to be prepared *to attend* to and *listen* to them and to attempt a working partnership. Thus the worker accepts that each person has worth, even when society is asking social workers to address what is viewed as unacceptable behaviour.

As regards younger people, this worker reported:

Younger people may have been rejected by a parent, accept no controls and show a very challenging behavioural style to their social worker. The *unconditional positive regard* of the worker can provide a contrast to the alienation and rejection experienced elsewhere. Social workers are sometimes misunderstood when they take this approach, as if they are approving the client's actions.

She gave as an example the social worker who received adverse publicity when she comforted the mother of one of the boys who was convicted of the sad death of James Bulger. After sentence was passed the practitioner involved was able to feel compassion for a woman whom she would have got to know while preparing court reports, a woman criticized by society as a parent and whose son was convicted of murder and sentenced to custody. This mother obviously remained a human being who experienced distress and needed support from social workers.

The practitioner continued:

There are opportunities for counselling that arise within the job, perhaps around a trauma; or specific issues that need resolution; or a programme to build self-confidence. The goals will be set but a counselling approach to achieving them can be taken. There is also opportunity for *empathic listening* and *support*. For example, I had one client who was self-referred for causing a minor injury to a child, for whom I was able to demonstrate unconditional positive regard. She was able to sense my *genuineness* and was helped by that to come to a decision to tackle her low self-esteem through psychotherapy. By accepting her worth as a fellow human being and not being afraid of her revelations of self-abuse, I saw her determination to sort out her life strengthen, though I had not the skill to take it further or the permission of the agency to do so. I saw her move on as my role ended because the children were not considered to be at risk.

This worker was able to articulate how she would accept the person and build on her strengths in a client-centred way, without compromising the authority, role or tasks required by the agency.

Empowerment

The concept of empowerment came into social work through writers such as Solomon (1976), writing on black communities in the USA. Empowerment has become a dominant theme in modern practice, reflecting a concern with the social inequalities and social exclusion faced by many of the client groups with whom practitioners work (Cochrane 1989; hooks 1991; Braye and Preston-Shoot 1995; Humphries 1996).

Empowerment in practice is complex because it encompasses values, ideologies, methods and outcomes, and because each individual has more or less power in different circumstances, in the same culture, at different times. Social workers therefore need to be critical and analytical in their approach to acting in an empowering way. It has been argued that an 'empowerment stategy requires commitment to both maintenance and improvement of effective equal services and also confrontation of pervasive negative valuations' (Payne 1992: 229). The aims of empowerment are to help clients to see:

- themselves as causal agents in finding solutions to their problems;
- social workers as having knowledge and skills that clients can use;
- social workers as peers and partners in solving problems;
- the power structure as complex and partly open to influence (Payne 1992: 230).

This leads to a model of practice that enables individuals to see themselves as having some control over their situation. The social worker's role becomes that of 'resources consultant, sensitiser and trainer' (Payne 1992: 230).

This role needs to be taken by the worker because communities and individuals internalize the 'negative valuations' of themselves that have accrued through experiences of oppression and disadvantage. A culture of 'power absence' rather than 'power failure' means people do not attempt to change the system. Social workers may collude with this if they concentrate change efforts on the individual rather than the structures which perpetuate disadvantage. Consciousness raising and radical and political advocacy approaches are needed to be effective. Seligman's (1975) work on learned helplessness is relevant here in arguing that if people constantly experience ineffectiveness as an outcome of their actions, then they will come to the view that there is no usefulness in their actions, and their ability to be motivated and solve problems will be impaired. There are times when social workers' empowerment stategies focus on working alongside individuals, who themselves advocate for their own rights.

It is important that social workers are clear what they mean when they talk about empowerment, because some of their work is within agencies that control resources, liberty or the right to bring up children. There can be confusion between a rhetorical expression of empowerment ideology and radical empowering practices in action. An uncritical approach to 'empowerment' may not be very different from *laissez-faire* or the 'get on your bike' approach, which believes that any individual can achieve his or her own solution unaided. It is therefore essential that empowerment aspirations are linked to advocacy practices and a clear understanding of rights.

Practice example: Antenna – providing counselling services for disabled people

This narrative account of an empowerment and advocacy approach to service provision comes from a practising social worker:

> The majority of services for disabled people have been, and still are, provided by non-disabled professionals.
>
> Due to lack of disability awareness and lack of personal experience of disability from non-disabled professionals, many disabled people have found these services to be delivered in a way which is patronizing, disempowering and inappropriate to their needs. Counselling is no exception.
>
> Through the growth of the disability movement, disabled people have identified a need for services provided and controlled by disabled people themselves, which not only increase the chances of being valued and understood as disabled people but also give credit to skills and experience that disabled people have themselves. This challenges the concept of disabled people only having a place as service users and brings to the fore the place for disabled people as professionals.
>
> Within the voluntary sector, projects where services are provided by disabled people have gradually emerged, though in terms of counselling services, there are still very few organizations across the country providing these within projects staffed and managed by disabled people.
>
> In Leicestershire, some years ago, a group of disabled people identified a need for counselling

services for disabled people provided by disabled people. They felt, through their own experiences and those of other disabled people they came into contact with, that there was a great need for disabled people to have access to counselling services. They also believed that counselling services provided by non-disabled professionals were often experienced as unhelpful because of a lack of attention to access needs and poor understanding of what it means to be disabled. Further, the view of disability from non-disabled professionals generally fell into the medical model rather than the social model of disability.

The social model of disability stresses the ways that disabled people are limited by the environment and by the barriers within society that prevent them from equal participation:

- lack of provision for access needs;
- lack of disability awareness;
- prevailing attitudes which mean disabled people are put down, disempowered and treated unequally;
- lack of equal access to social, educational and employment opportunities.

If these issues are not taken into account and clearly acknowledged in providing counselling services, then counselling puts the onus back on disabled people and the 'problem' becomes wholly personal rather than social.

There is an important balance to be achieved in counselling where both social and personal aspects of disability are recognized. This means that neither the social aspects such as lack of access and disability awareness, nor the personal aspects such as sexuality, pain and loss, are ignored.

Antenna is a voluntary organization which has provided counselling services for disabled people since January 1996. It is a project managed and staffed by disabled people. In consulting with people who use or have used the service and our members,

this has been identified as the most important
aspect of the project.

(Liz Mackenzie, Antenna Coordinator 1998)

Empowerment and the Community Care Act

The tensions between empowerment philosophy and the practice of social work are seen clearly in the implementation of
the NHS and Community Care Act 1990. In the early stages of
implementation the tensions between resources shortfall and the
concept of needs-led assessment and intervention have been a
constant theme of discussion. Browne (1996) specifies the short-
falls: the extent to which users are informed and included in the
process; deficits in recording agreements in writing; and administrative procedures being difficult for users to comprehend. Deakin
(1996) agrees that the empowerment focus has been undermined
by under-resourcing (with delays undercutting principles of user
choice), problems of definition and procedural obstacles (Whose
needs are to be met, user or carer? What if these conflict?) and
service user choice (How can a user have choice when contracts
are awarded in a quasi-market controlled by managers?). Deakin
concludes that 'the user is not at the centre of the picture in
community care practice.'

In this climate, speaking cynically, social workers are almost
reduced to using their personal communication skills to 'say no
nicely'. This would be unethical and need not be so. Workers
need their interpersonal communication skills not only to enable
users to express their agenda but also to use verbal skills in
challenge and advocacy in order to obtain a needed resource.

Counselling skills for empowerment

The notion that self-directed solutions to individual problems
are best achieved by the client with a supporter is as central to
empowering social work practice as it is to counselling practice.
Social workers operate within the overt and covert power structures that agencies embody. There is a creative, challenging and
stressful tension between agency role and public expectation.

Counsellors mislead themselves if they think that without a powerful bureaucracy around them, they are not themselves powerful. The counsellor is usually perceived as an 'expert' and in possession of knowledge and resources, such as the power to give or withhold help, offer long or short contracts and make referrals.

In any helping interaction, awareness of the dynamics of actual and perceived power is necessary. Failure to recognize the subtle and explicit dimensions of power is potentially detrimental to the client. Within social work agencies practitioners can use interpersonal skills to build relationships and practise in a way which promotes and enables as far as is possible within the limitations of the agency's remit. It is also possible to use skills of advocacy and challenge to work patiently and persistently with users to build up self-esteem and achieve their aims within family systems and communities. In addition to personal work with individuals, social workers are able to intervene and broker resources in support of the actions and endeavours of clients achieving their goals.

Practice example

The following narrative shows a practitioner using counselling, advocacy and other skills to facilitate a learning disabled woman to achieve her and her family's goal, so that she could begin to take an active role in the community beyond the immediate family. This intervention to increase the life experience and social opportunities of an adult with learning disabilities is typical of much work undertaken in this sector of adult services.

The practitioner was responding to a referral from a GP to a social services department. Jean Harris had previously been referred to the department with a view to obtaining some daytime activities for her. The family's attempts to obtain services had not progressed beyond the duty desk. Thus the system had blocked access to resources which offered opportunities to Jean. The family had engaged the advocacy and power of their GP, who insisted that their second request for help was allocated a practitioner. The worker identified how Jean, in requesting services, had met delay and prejudiced beliefs about her abilities. This led to low expectations, opportunity deprivation, negative and diminished experience, more delay and therefore negative self-evaluation and expectations. In other words, she experienced disempowerment and learned helplessness, as identified by Solomon and Seligman.

The practitioner decided to use systems theory as a framework for understanding her client, but also considered models of disability, transitions theory, normalization principles, empowerment principles and ego psychology. Her major aim was to promote Jean's right to the choice of a service which met her needs and enabled her to participate in society in a way which was satisfying for her, building on her strengths and interests. The practitioner therefore undertook an assessment of need within the framework of the Community Care Act 1990 to find ways of enabling the user and family to achieve the desired outcome.

The practitioner began the first interview with the conscious exercise of *empathy* to discover how Jean viewed herself and her environment. Initially, this meant *listening* to the anger of Ida Harris, Jean's mother, who was annoyed at the way the previous request for daycare had resulted in unhelpful advice and no service provision. Faced with a general complaint, the practitioner *summarized to reflect back at a feeling level* the dejection and frustration this had produced in the family. She gave some time to the *ventilation of feelings* and *actively listened* to make *accurate responses*, with *summaries* that showed *accurate empathy*. She followed this by clarifying the reasons for the agency's past response (service review), but also made it clear that a complaint could be made and how this could be done.

A relationship was built which led to an introduction to the whole family, which consisted of six extended members. At this stage the client herself was quiet (*attention to body language*) and did not reply when gently addressed. The practitioner first *listened attentively* to the expressed thoughts and feelings of the family, who expressed a view that Jean was supported within a close and loving family, but had little experience to develop outside of it. She had been to school independently, but now the parents chose to provide transport everywhere she went. She had a brief spell of work experience but this was supervised by a sister. Jean had never attended a college and did not go anywhere alone. The family had been encouraged by their GP to think about the future and to enable their daughter to socialize outside of the family system. The practitioner, having *listened*, supported this view. By the end of the interview she had managed, through the mother, to gather that Jean enjoyed dancing and cooking.

Jean had no recent experience outside her family network, and had expressed to the family her concerns about being 'different from other people'. The practitioner had established some rapport with Ida Harris but wanted to establish communication with Jean to *check out* her view of her situation. She also thought it possible that Jean had a negative self-valuation, and aimed to enable her to find her equal rights as an adult person. This meant support and self-image building. The worker therefore tried to encourage Jean to speak for herself within interviews. This also meant both *challenge* to the family members and much use of *encouraging body language* and *minimal prompts*.

Once communication with Jean herself was achieved, the practitioner learnt how a previous attempt to visit a day centre had been unhappy and that the consequences were not worked through, thus blocking Jean's willingness to consider it again. The practitioner therefore stated and restated to Jean that she would be able to say no to anything she did not want to do, *advocating* within the family for her right to choose. She used *jargon-free language*, such as 'You need only have a look to see if you like it' and 'You will decide if you want to go.'

The worker researched community resources and found a drop-in facility with a relaxed group atmosphere, based in a local bungalow, attended by a few others. From there opportunities arose to branch out to local courses and activities. Jean turned this down and the worker accepted her right to choose. The focus turned to her interests in cooking and dancing. There was a cookery course at a local college, but a series of delays and administrative blocks, which considerably engaged the practitioner's advocacy skills, made it difficult to make arrangements for a trial visit. Meanwhile, a visit by bus to the college was made with Jean so that she could see what it was like. Contact was maintained by brief visits to the family home.

During her direct conversations with Jean she used *open-ended questions and paraphrasing to check meanings and maintain the relationship* (and *accepted pauses and silence*). Jean shared her interest in cooking at home with the worker. Eventually a place on the cookery course for people with special needs was available and the client was enabled to attend on her own. She enjoyed it and expressed the wish to continue. This was a huge step, as it was her first social activity outside the family since leaving school. A second planned step was to attend a creative arts group in a small college within walking distance of the family home.

The worker invested considerable time in the work, using *empathy* and *linking* to gain understanding and to frame communications to Jean and her family. The practitioner surmised that the client was feeling labelled and that both she and her family were perceiving her in a disabling way. Jean expressed her dissatisfaction and frustration by refusing to speak to family members, often for long periods. The worker had to use *empathy* and *communication skills* to build trust and engage the client directly to establish her genuine needs and feelings.

Berne's (1961) model of parent–adult–child interactions was used to try to change the interactions between Jean and her family from parent–child to a more adult–adult model. A major part of this was *modelling* through practitioner interactions in an adult–adult style, focusing on Jean's strengths and rights. An understanding of *defences* helped the practitioner *to clarify* that Jean was anxious about visiting new places because of a previous bad experience where she had not been told she was only 'going for a look' and believed she was going to be 'left there'. This information only emerged when the worker took time to *listen* to Jean's anxiety and gently to *explore* it through *open questions*. In her work to 'promote and enable', the practitioner gave constant attention to *affirming the client's communications* and encouraging her to assert her views. This was only possible through the understanding and partnership built with the family, who, after the initial hostility, became positive about the service received and derived benefit from the *ventilation* and *acceptance* of some of their frustrations.

This example shows how skilled personal interactions build trust to promote and enable a service user to take small but crucial steps towards fulfilling her goals and lessening her frustrations. Jean was also enabled to build on her strengths. Through careful, planned interventions it was possible to work without conflict to promote the rights of both Jean and her family. Through the worker's activity resolutions were found that a previous more bureaucratic response had failed to provide.

Empowerment and advocacy in social work are enabled through counselling skills. Neville (1996) has developed a grid model for social work process in empowerment. It is designed as a working tool for practitioners, but states clearly that its usefulness is in 'giving a framework for analysing how a piece of work is done'. It cannot be an objective test of the achievement of empowering practice because 'the client is the only person who can determine that themselves.'

The framework identifies:

- areas of clients' lives where they wish to acquire power;
- the areas of access that social workers need to offer in order to enable people to acquire power in these identified areas;
- the support that needs to be offered by agencies or workers for the access to become effective;
- the social work skills that are required to offer effective support to clients, in order to acquire power over areas of their lives, including *listening, empathy, advocacy, respect, counselling, antioppressive practice, user involvement, negotiation* and *conciliation*.

This grid is the outcome of considerable research with agencies, social work practioners, training courses, users and student groups. The full grid is included in the Appendix.

Practice example
Working with the strengths of individuals in an empowering way is harder to achieve when social workers need to act to protect someone from risk of danger, from himself or herself or from others. The following example shows the dilemmas of ethical practice, but the workers' counselling skills and personal approach are still in evidence, while they are using legal powers to protect the children.

A parent had left her two small children, aged three and five, in the care of her elderly parents and apparently disappeared for several months. Prior to this event, social workers had worked to support both parents to care for the children in their own rented accommodation. The children's father had received a prison sentence for offences related to drugs and was therefore now unable to care for them. Monitoring the impact of the parent's substance use and lifestyle on the children had previously been an intermittent concern.

The grandparents contacted social services because they were no longer in good health, and were finding the responsibility of the two small children more than they could really manage. The father apparently had no relatives who might help to care for the children. The mother returned, took the children with her and left her parents' home. She moved with them from friend to friend, as she and her partner had been evicted from their former house.

She finally returned to her parents, clearly without resources or a home, and probably using substances. She then left the children again after a week's stay. After another week the elderly grandparents asked social services to accommodate the children. Support services were offered, but to no avail. The children were therefore placed with short-term foster carers. After a few weeks the mother returned, resumed contact and then removed the children from foster care (as was her right, since they were voluntarily accommodated).

She began moving from friend to friend again, until the police found her by the roadside late one night, with no resources, possibly using substances and with the children in a neglected condition. The children were returned to the foster carers, but this time emergency protection orders were obtained. Subsequently, a decision was made to promote the rights and welfare of the children by applying for interim care orders and assessing their long-term future. It was considered increasingly important to ensure some stability for the children. They were old enough for day nursery and school and were showing behavioural signs of distress, as well as experiencing physical neglect.

At this stage, another relative, the mother's sister (previously unknown to social services), came forward to offer care. She had her own home, had older children and was willing to help. She and her family were assessed, and the children were placed with her with the back-up of orders and social work supervision. At this stage the mother's whereabouts were not known, but the father, who was in custody, was agreeable to this arrangement. The parents' right to contact was maintained but when the mother returned she was angry about the removal of the children and the existence of the court orders.

Efforts were made, unsuccessfully, by social services to support the mother to establish a permanent base for her children. While the children appeared resilient, their former lifestyle had affected them. They needed continued stability of care at home and school. They appeared to have settled happily in the extended family setting. They remained in touch with their grandparents and their mother on an occasional basis.

The skills needed in establishing this work to 'promote and enable' the children's right to a secure upbringing were many. Legal and administrative knowledge was essential, as was a sound knowledge of the needs and rights of both parents and children. Work in this framework of statutory functions also required a high order of interpersonal communication skills.

First, the social workers had the task of *attentive listening* to all the adults involved, without compromising the child-centred approach. The Children Act requires social workers to work in partnership with parents and other kin as far as possible, while promoting the well-being of children. Second, the skill of *paraphrasing responses* to the adults was needed, which included the communication of some contested decisions. Here they used *reflecting back* and *immediacy* to check that each party was clear about the reasons for the actions of the social workers.

The task of collecting information to make an assessment needed skills in *questioning*, with the use of *alternatives to questions* to explore options. The skills of *confronting and challenging* the parent's belief in her ability to meet the children's needs in such a way that partnership and contact were retained were essential. In this situation, despite the care with which the workers tried to maintain a partnership with the mother and grandmother, the mother was angry because of the care orders. The grandmother also became alienated by the legal action, despite the fact that she had initially requested assistance. The grandmother needed help in accepting that she was unable through illness to care for her grandchildren, and decisive action was needed to secure a more settled lifestyle for the children. Skills in *working with and containing strong feelings*, allowing some *ventilation*, were used. The father was engaged in the process and his views were sought. He was *facilitated to express* his concerns.

Throughout the work the practitioners chose to take a person-centred approach, without compromising the child-centred focus of practice, by understanding that all the people in this family had worth in themselves and could interpret their own lives in ways that were valid and worthwhile. However, they also acknowledged that the agency view, of the mother's incapacity to care for the children consistently, challenged this. Thus, in the clear decision to enable and promote the children's right to an education and to be free from risk, at least two of the adults experienced distress and disempowerment.

This example is included to acknowledge the difficulties of the situations in which counselling skills are employed in social work practice. Care has to be taken not to use skills to manipulate or persuade or to give false assurances. At all stages there has to be honesty about events and intended actions, with areas of disagreement as clearly identified as possible. None the less, careful and ethical use of counselling skills can facilitate the necessary interactions and make the needed negotiations clear and unambiguous.

In this work acceptance of the person and a non-judgemental approach to the difficulties the parents were experiencing was important. Difficult decisions had to be made to provide alternative care for the children, until their parents were in a better position to bring them up. It was important to keep the possibility of the parents resuming care alive in the minds of the workers, children and extended family. A placement within the extended family was thought to be less likely to cause permanent loss of attachment to their origins for the children than foster care with strangers.

Skills such as the *ability to be empathic, to tolerate strong and hostile feelings, to communicate honestly and clearly, paraphrasing, summarizing* and *checking meanings, understanding defences, splitting* and *projection* were all in evidence. Responding to the anger and distress of parents when difficult decisions have to be made is a very skilled process. The principles of the Children Act 1989 are that whenever children are separated from parents, social workers have to be involved in maintaining positive contact and supporting the parents to regain care of their children, wherever this can be achieved, without significantly harming the children's health and development. Sometimes decisive action to separate children from parents who are harming them has to be taken and communicated unambiguously.

Similar constraints surround the concept of empowerment and advocacy in mental and health and criminal justice settings, where skills are harnessed to the primary tasks of care in the community and tackling offending behaviour and its consequences.

Voluntary and community agencies are often better placed to use counselling skills in empowerment and for advocacy purposes. Agencies are often set up and funded precisely to ensure that advocacy services are available to those affected by the legal intervention of the state. Counselling skills can also be used in community activity to facilitate change.

> *Practice example*
> This example comes from a written account of a consultation forum. Pushpa Gandhi (1996) describes an 'innovative open space forum where older people could express their needs without being intimidated by professionals.' Working from an empowerment philosophy, Liverpool social services set up a consultation forum for older people in an ethnic minority community to be able to express their views about the services they wanted. Using the mechanism of small groups working on an 'open' participation system, people were able to express their views and so *be listened to*. Gandhi (1996: 13) concludes that the main messages she understood from this work were:
>
> - if we want partnership in the true sense then we must go out and find ways to communicate with service users, carers and representatives;
> - even with so much research and written literature devoted to improving services for ethnic minority groups, they are still struggling to receive help for their basic needs;
> - we can empower service users only when we listen to them and integrate their wishes in future policy and planning (anything else is lip service);
> - even if nothing comes out of this forum, it made service users and professionals aware of their needs and of the gaps in our present system.

Advocacy

Advocacy is the activity which may follow an understanding of the client's wishes in order to achieve their fulfilment. Advocacy may be used to help someone obtain something from another person or institution with more power. The practitioner may use his or her own power and influence in the interest of the real expressed wishes of another. Bateman (1995) describes advocacy as a 'sequential activity based on learned skills'. Social workers frequently undertake advocacy activities for clients to ensure that other agencies meet their responsibilities. Bateman (1995: 25–41) usefully offers six principles for advocacy:

- act in the client's best interests;
- act in accordance with the client's wishes and instructions;
- keep the client properly informed;
- carry out instructions with diligence and competence;
- act impartially and offer frank, independent advice;
- maintain the rule of confidentiality.

In these activities, as others, the practitioner will find it useful to listen carefully, to be skilled in using questions, to be able to respond accurately and clearly and to be aware of the non-verbal aspects of communication.

Conclusion

The message is clear that professionals who seek to promote and enable, to empower, to work to user strengths and to advocate must first effectively use their listening and responding and linked counselling skills before moving to enactment. Failure to use these counselling skills in the processes of social work may contribute to mismatches between service request and outcome, and the gap between the aspirations to empowerment and the failure to achieve it. Accurate advocacy is based on accurate listening and responding.

Chapter 4

To assess and plan: relevant counselling skills

Assessment in social work is the foundation of planning and decision making. It is a cornerstone of professional activity in health, education, voluntary sector provision, social services, housing, benefits agencies and other services available to the public. Assessments may be made briefly on the telephone or may be extended and comprehensive. Assessments are used to plan work and to assist professional and user decision making. CCETSW recognizes this by requiring that beginning practitioners show the ability to:

> Work in partnership to assess and review people's circumstances and plan responses to need and risk.
>
> (CCETSW 1995)

Assessments are usually guided by written frameworks. It can be argued that the key components of such frameworks should be:

- underpinned by knowledge from research, literature and practice;
- evidence-based, particularly related to human development, family functioning and the environment in which the person lives;
- built on concepts of need which are relevant, holistic and person-centred;

- congruent with the principles of relevant legislation;
- explicit about the theories, models and methods used;
- capable of being developed and evaluated.

Social work activity comprises cycles of assessment, intervention and evaluation in which goals are identified, methods used and resources mobilized. These cycles take place within legal, organizational and ethical boundaries. Assessment is the first stage of a process aimed at achieving specified outcomes and not, as it sometimes has become in practice, an end in itself. It is also important to understand that the process of assessment may, by the way it is undertaken, contribute to the achievement of outcomes. Several theories and models have influenced current practice. These are now discussed briefly.

The origins of social work assessment

Early casework writing borrowed from medicine and devised the concept of 'social diagnosis' (Richmond 1922; Hollis 1964). This model for assessment, which concentrated on the individual, remained in general use until the early 1970s, but increasingly there began to emerge a recognition that individuals were influenced by their social circumstances. Haines (1975) describes social work assessment as 'the ability to assess a social situation and intervene in whatever seems to be the most effective way.' He conceptualizes the social work process as 'assessment, action and evaluation', in which the purpose of assessment is: 'to gather as much information as possible about the situation and form some opinion about its meaning for the client and its implications for action' (Haines 1975: 16).

Haines's work was taken further in the late 1970s by Curnock and Hardiker (1979). Assessment is conceptualized as a filter by which practitioners weigh and sift information to plan their interventions. The stages in the assessment are described as follows:

- acquisition of information;
- studying facts and feelings;
- balancing and formulating;
- strategies in goal setting;
- intervention.

Curnock and Hardiker's model of assessment is constructed from empirical research with practitioners in probation, childcare and mental health settings, formulating practice which has been observed and analysed. They also define the elements of the assessment as:

- frameworks;
- communication;
- balance sheets of risks;
- needs and resources;
- goal setting strategies (Curnock and Hardiker 1979: 162).

They suggest that these phases overlap and that assessment is not a static function. Assessment is informed by paradigms (or theory frameworks) which guide the practitioner. Interview schedules are devised which reflect these.

Compton and Galaway (1989) develop further the concept of assessment through their classic text, *Social Work Processes*, which makes a major contribution to social work theory and practice. They suggest that 'the ultimate purpose of assessment is to contribute the understanding necessary for appropriate planning' (Compton and Galaway 1989: 414). The phases of assessment are described as:

- purpose and process;
- doing the assessment;
- exploring the problem;
- putting meaning to the situation;
- feelings and facts.

These areas are explored and linked to social work activities. The framework produces a helpful practical tool for practitioners.

Similar assessment frameworks have been developed by Pincus and Minahan (1973), Specht and Vickery (1977), Coulshed (1991) and Meyer (1993). These are widely cited in social work literature and continue to be applied to a range of tasks (Taylor and Devine 1993; Thompson 1995; Sinclair *et al.* 1995). These frameworks are essentially about ways in which practitioners interact with the public to gather relevant information and formulate, with service users, ways of achieving specified outcomes.

However, while the principle of undertaking
has been well established, the purposes and theory
developed in different directions. The main shift in
of assessment since 1970 has been a move away f.⌐⌐⌐ ⌐ ⌐⌐⌐₀
nostic focus towards understanding the perspectives of the client
within a holistic and needs-led framework (White and Epston
1989; Meyer 1993; Lloyd and Taylor 1995). These approaches
build on the identified strengths of individuals rather than looking for dysfunction. They emphasize assessing what is present in
terms of the client's strengths and establishing successful ways
of problem solving (de Shazer 1985). In some models, the users'
narratives or stories determine the process (Franklin and Jordan
1995; Laird 1995).

There appears to be a spectrum of models of assessment,
from diagnosis of dysfunction through problem solving to the
designation of clients as 'expert' about their own situation. The
existence of different approaches, each with its own advocates,
sets up a tension between diagnostic (exclusion/pathology) and
social (inclusion/strengths) approaches to assessment that may be
spurious. In practice, the use of different approaches may relate
more to the context of assessment and its purpose than to the
framework *per se*.

Current social work practice is concerned with two pre-
dominating approaches: risk assessment and needs-led assessment.

The preoccupation with risk assessment

So far the emergence of different approaches to assessment has
been applied generally to social work activity. However, in relation to assessing children and their families, there has been a
preoccupation over the past twenty years with models for risk
assessment that has tended to stress family dysfunction rather
than strengths. This is understandable, because since the death
of Maria Colwell in 1973, public anxiety about preventing child
deaths has permeated practitioners' perceptions of their role in a
fundamental way. Highly publicized 'failures' to protect children
from danger have led the professions to develop checklists of
indicators and predictors which claim to measure the safety of a
child within a family.

Similarly, there has been concern in adult services about the safety of vulnerable groups of older or disabled people and concern about the 'risks to themselves and dangerousness' of some people with mental illness. The Probation Service has been concerned to assess better the risk to the public from the release into community supervision of some offenders. Consequently, much attention has been given to the development of scales to assess: the risks to children from parental dangerousness; the risks offenders pose to the community; the risks some adults pose to themselves and others (Kempshall and Pritchard 1996; Prins 1995; Home Office 1997).

Risk assessment scales, at their present stage of development and implementation, offer a range of predictors and factors derived from what in the past has contributed to dangerous actions. They provide a map of clusters of factors which, when aggregated, indicate cause for concern. The deficit of this approach is that, despite increasing sophistication in the ability to devise scales and evaluate them, the variables involved and their inter-relationships are so complex that any decision making requires a high level of professional judgement and qualitative assessment. There is literature to assist with this decision making (Schon 1983; Dowie and Elstein 1988; Schaffer 1990; Lindsey 1994; Yelloly and Henkel 1995).

The *Framework for the Assessment of Children in Need and their Families* (Department of Health 2000), which will be widely used by children and family social workers, takes a developmental approach to assessment that considers the child within a wider context. However, to use such a framework well and undertake complex assessments, social workers need to be equipped with a range of skills in asking questions, gathering information and responding, to facilitate the best outcomes for the people with whom they work.

Practice example

A social worker is described using counselling skills to facilitate a social work assessment in relation to a teenager. Sophie (13) had been diagnosed as suffering from anorexia nervosa. Since she was 11 she had been showing symptoms of this illness. She was referred to social services because the clinician who was seeing her thought she was at risk of neglect. Her parents did not seem able to help her to retain her weight gain after she was discharged from the inpatient clinic. A social work assessment was requested.

The focus of the social worker's assessment was initially with the parents to consider their capacities for care, their management of their daughter's situation and the general family relationships. A feature of Sophie's situation, already identified, was substantial jealousy of her four-year-old sister. At the time that the social work assessment was taking place, Sophie's therapy continued with her NHS specialist.

The initial phase of the assessment was to compile a family history. This was a time-consuming task and needed patience and persistence on the part of the worker to gain information that was relevant. These parents were likely to be feeling sensitive to the potential implication of 'blame' for their child's situation, rather than seeing the assessment as an opportunity to understand past events and plan for change. Their feelings therefore needed to be understood and contained by the practitioner.

To keep the users engaged with the process, the worker chose to start with *active listening, paraphrasing, summarizing* and *using closed and opened questions* to check information and to explore. The practitioner felt it was important to remain open-minded and accepting. At this stage, decisions about which techniques to use affected what information was given and by whom. If the worker had interrupted too often or focused too soon she might have closed down the parents' narrative and missed important information. At the same time a gentle *focus, using summary and paraphrase,* was needed to avoid repetition and becoming stuck on points in a time-consuming way. This required skill and judgement, alongside awareness of the potential selectivity of the process.

Once this was done, the next stage was to use *non-critical acceptance* to set the scene for greater understanding of the impact of certain relationships and behaviours on family functioning. This stance was important because if the parents had felt judged, they might have become defensive and less open to considering options for change. As the process developed, the practitioner *challenged* the couple in respect of the way they were focusing outside the family to scapegoat and blame the agencies involved for Sophie's difficulties. The worker began making *links* between some of their past experiences and behaviours and current ways of parenting their daughters, to assist them with exploring future ways of addressing issues such as rivalry between the two children.

At this stage the practitioner's therapeutic approach to assessment 'crashed' because service managers, at the instigation of the clinician involved, started to consider legal proceedings as a way to 'make' the family care more appropriately for Sophie. The practitioner made an argument against this by saying that it did not seem right to take the family to court at this stage. This view was supported by her immediate managers, but led to a loss of confidence between the clinician and the local authority. However, the outcome was clinical care being taken over locally and a less coercive approach being adopted.

The function of the assessment had been to clarify the approach, which became the basis for planning with new clinicians, the family and social services. Counselling skills such as *empathic understanding* and *genuineness* enabled the practitioner to maintain a working alliance with the family in the face of many challenges to its continuance. However, *challenging* and *confrontation* were seen as vital in asking the family to look at their dynamics. The worker had emphasized that in their future work with therapists they would need to work honestly with their issues if they were to achieve change and understanding that could benefit their daughter.

This kind of assessment, undertaken within a legal framework, required finely tuned personal skills. Reliance on assessment procedures alone would not have enabled them to build a working alliance with the family in a way that led to a less intrusive intervention in keeping with the Children Act 1989.

Re-evaluating risk assessment

Recent literature has indicated the beginnings of some disaffection with this approach to the welfare of children because of the problem of undifferentiated data (Wald and Woolverton 1990; English and Pecora 1994; Corby 1996). Lyons *et al.* (1996) review ten risk assessment models and their usefulness. They appear to endorse the caution sounded by Corby, and conclude that further model development is needed. Likewise, Gaudin *et al.* (1996) conclude that models for risk assessment are still not developed enough to be more than useful in guiding the management of individual cases. Corby (1996: 27) concludes:

> considerable attention has been paid to the context in which child protection assessments are carried out at both macro and micro levels. It has been emphasised that at the macro level there is still great uncertainty about the extent to which the state should intervene in families to protect children. This is a value laden issue that will not be resolved by the development of more scientific approaches to risk assessment. At the micro level, perhaps because of societal ambivalence, there are many barriers to conducting assessments as rationally and comprehensively as many professionals would like.
>
> (Corby 1996: 27)

American literature has identified another set of problems of risk assessment: inadequate implementation and difficulties in evaluation (Doueck *et al.* 1992; Murphy Berman 1994). Risk assessment procedures are seen to vary on a number of dimensions, are complex to compare against each other and need to take account of variables such as the purpose of the assessment and the nature of the decisions to be made.

The Australian picture is similar. A study from 1989 concludes that risk indicators provide a framework for assessment which can eliminate much idiosyncratic decision making. But

:ators can be 'perfect predictors' or 'capture the whole' sh and Drew 1989). Dalgleish (1997, in press) takes this work ~orward by evaluating eight risk assessment models and developing a further model which separates the analysis of risk from the judgement about what is an acceptable degree of risk, and from subsequent decision making. The experience, expectations, motivations and history of the social worker are considered to 'make explicit aspects of the judgements and decisions made by child protection workers in uncertain and risky situations.' This work is a valuable contribution to clarifying the issues of implementation and training for professionals using risk assessment scales.

Overall, checklists are helpful mapping tools in decision making, but they cannot be definitive. The conclusion from the literature is that reasoned and balanced professional judgements carefully made by those with 'quality' and skill remain crucial. The strengths of risk assessment scales are in providing a rational framework for the collation of data that predicts dangerousness. The deficits are that, despite increasing sophistication in their design and evaluation, the variables for assessing children in the context of their families are so complex that professional judgement underpinned by theory and research still remains the cornerstone of best practice.

Such tasks with children and adults can only be undertaken by a professional who is legally competent, and has empowering attitudes and interpersonal skills in gathering information, in weighing it and in agreeing plans with users and other professionals. Judgements have to be made in personal areas about parenting, and the abilities of family members to sustain and provide for each other with or without external intervention. Here, the human development-based person-centred understandings, on the one hand, and the verbal abilities which derive from psychological counselling approaches, on the other hand, remain essential.

Practice example

This example describes a worker undertaking an assessment of risk using the Department of Health guidelines. While the assessment is about risk, the empowering approach of the worker is useful within a context where role authority is fully used. This example typifies the assessments social workers routinely make in relation to unexplained injuries which have occurred to small children.

The Department of Health recommends that at the beginning of an assessment there is a dialogue between the social worker and the parents to confirm there is a shared understanding. Parents need to be aware of processes and potential outcomes. They need to know what will happen to information they give and on what basis judgements and decisions may be made. This requires knowledge and confidence from the worker as well as skills in *clarity of communication* and *an ability to convey information with both empathy and authority.*

An assessment of a small child and her two parents was undertaken because an injury to the child, Jenny, aged two, could not be explained. The local authority was unsure as to what risk might be posed to this child if she stayed in the care of her parents. She had experienced a potentially serious injury but there had been no police investigation so far. The immediate concern was to ensure Jenny's safety and welfare.

The worker decided that the most empowering approach was to be frank. Using the skill of *immediacy*, she openly acknowledged that the process would mean the parents looking at hitherto private areas of their lives, and that this might feel intrusive and difficult. This approach led to the couple sharing the feelings they were currently experiencing (*open-ended questions, ventilation of feelings*) about aspects of their involvement with child protection agencies (the close monitoring of their physical care of their child by health visitors). This *immediacy* on the part of the worker led to a relationship which was more akin to the partnership approach promoted in the Children Act. The worker's *empathy* to feelings, even though the close monitoring had to continue, opened up the way for an honesty about feelings and process that would enhance the future of the assessment.

The worker was given permission by the agency to accept the lack of evidence about how the injury happened, and to move on to assessing the strengths and positive factors within the family, as well as identifying problems and concerns. A plan would then be drawn up for future action. To explore the parenting capacity and abilities of the mother and father of the child, two social workers conducted individual interviews with each parent. The worker with the father considered it important to be an *empathic listener* to facilitate the process. For example, when he shared some of the difficulties he had experienced during his adolescence, the practitioner *reflected back* that this could be understood and related to his own parenting style. Providing a therapeutic understanding, while remaining in the role of assessor, made the worker acutely conscious of gender dynamics and the need to resolve power dynamics. The worker endeavoured to enable the parents to consider the close monitoring of physical care of the child as a way of demonstrating their abilities, so that close scrutiny could later be reduced.

The worker continued to balance the assessment of risk factors, such as the parents' personal histories and current socio-economic position, with the responsibility to protect Jenny from harm, while, if possible, maintaining her in her family home. The social workers endeavoured to keep an open relationship, without colluding or compromising their concerns. This involved considering the possible risk posed by:

- the mother's history of care and her history of depression and anxiety;
- the father's use of alcohol from time to time;
- the stress caused by financial hardship;
- the presence of some arguments and violence between the parents;
- the pressures of professional surveillance;
- the presence of two small siblings, putting pressure on the mother's time.

Practical measures, such as obtaining grants for furniture and day nursery places for the two younger children, were offered, alongside personal support for the parents. Discussion was undertaken of the impact of identified risk factors on current parenting with the family. The decision was taken to maintain Jenny at home, with support and continued monitoring. The role of assessor gave the worker considerable power both to intervene in a supportive way and to take action to remove Jenny if needed.

The practitioner concluded:

> It has been suggested that child protection has become inexplicably linked with control. This view portrays aspects of the child protection role which challenge traditional notions of social work as a helping profession. The dilemmas faced while working with this family illustrate the difficulty workers can experience in attempting to rationalize the use of power within an approach which aspires to partnership with parents.

Children and family social workers should never lose sight of the need to make sure that children are safe and protected from potential harm. However, it is possible to use interpersonal skills to facilitate the process without compromising role or authority. These workers used their abilities to build a partnership approach which helped to assess the child's safety and work with the adults on their parenting abilities.

Assessment in community care social work

The NHS and Community Care Act 1990 resulted in a major shift of emphasis in services for vulnerable adults. The practice guidelines set out for the first time a model consistent with the social work processes of collation, collection and analysis of information. The guidelines make clear that the emphasis is on needs-led assessment, not fitting clients to services. Guidance from government says that local authorities have a duty to 'assess people's needs holistically in relation to a wide range of possible service options, rather than having separate service-led assessments' (Department of Health 1991a). The assessment principles as specified in the practitioner's guide are to: 'negotiate the scope of assessment; choose the setting; clarify expectations; promote participation; establish a relationship of trust; assess need; determine eligibility; set priorities; agree objectives; record the assessment' (Department of Health 1991b). The implementation of this has produced some tensions and contradictions for practitioners.

The debate about need

There has been continuous debate about what is needs-led. For example, is need disadvantage, or the right to a minimum level of provision, such as clean water, adequate nutrition, adequate protection and housing, a non-hazardous work environment, appropriate health care, security in childhood, significant primary relationships, physical security, appropriate education, safer birth control and child bearing (Doyal and Gough 1991)? Alternatively, need has been understood to encompass all the dimensions in Bradshaw's (1972) taxonomy: normative needs, felt needs, expressed needs, comparative needs. The literature is preoccupied with questions such as: what is need and who defines it; to what extent is the system needs-led? It is also suggested that unmet needs are seldom well collated and that the link between population needs and individual needs is not well documented (Percy-Smith 1996).

Differential approaches to assessment

Differential approaches to assessment have been taken by various stakeholders. Assessment may be identified by managers as an important area of practice that should lead to more effective use of limited resources. Practitioners may see assessment as a means of responding to client need. Users and carers may be unclear about the function of assessment. There is some confusion around the concept that assessments should match needs and resources, while not being led by existing resource provision. Concern is expressed that assessment becomes a tool for rationing (Powell and Goddard 1996).

Centrally or locally defined models?

In the absence of centrally determined models that specify needs in relation to particular policy areas and set out optimum or minimum standards of provision, it is argued that it is difficult to see how equity between geographical areas can be achieved (Percy-Smith 1996: 64). At the time of implementation, a group of 11 local authorities took a different view and wrote that, 'in reflecting on the experience of working together on the implementation of assessment and care management, participants concluded that there was no substitute for authorities devising solutions in the light of their own particular circumstances and experiences. Recognizing the need to develop local approaches was very important' (Beardshaw 1991). A balance has to be sought between central policy directives and local autonomy.

Interdisciplinary boundaries

The boundary between social care and health care remains contentious (Browne 1996), with implications for the effectiveness of interdisciplinary work. The identification of the involvement of different disciplines does not necessarily lead to an integrated service. Thus the social worker undertaking an assessment has to consider the relationships between legal framework, procedural guidelines, eligibility criteria, local resources and social work approaches to helping.

Social workers must listen carefully to expressed need and use verbal skills to advocate for the most fitting service for their user group. It may be argued that service-led provision is both costly and time-consuming. However, if users are appraised about options carefully they will not abandon services they agreed to because they felt unable to say no or were pressurized into acceptance. If hasty plans are made as a result of failure to interview carefully, the time taken up by complaints, renegotiation and wastage will be more expensive than the extra time taken to listen carefully and provide a needs-led response in the first place.

Social workers in adult services say that they can use their interpersonal skills effectively to balance the needs and resources equation which the legislation has mandated for local authorities.

They also meet families in times of crisis in their lives, which means counselling skills are often needed to facilitate the work.

Practice example

However good the guidelines for practice, human situations are often more complicated than procedural manuals can accommodate. This means practitioners have to take a flexible and holistic approach to implementation. The example which follows comes from an experienced adult services practitioner.

> We cannot divorce people and their significant relationships from the task in hand. They are interrelated. A tangled relationship will very often impede the way to a useful outcome to an assessment. A healthy relationship will more often than not facilitate the process. In all work I found myself using some counselling skills. With some relationships the use of a wide range of counselling skills was needed to facilitate the moving forward of the assessment.
>
> There were occasions when I would set out on the assessment with a carer to begin to gather facts, when the carer's experience of stress, loss, frustration and anger would overwhelm them. At this point I would set down the fact finding task and give time, using *counselling skills* to allow *expression of feeling* and offloading. I would very often find that in validating the experience in this way some trust was built and the task of assessment could proceed (*ventilation of feelings, acceptance, attentive listening, minimal prompts, clarifying, removing blocks, understanding defences, and reactions to loss*).
>
> I would offer carers a separate interview. Sometimes people would take this up with the specific purpose of exploring their role as carers. This was very often a kind of counselling session, and change would come about as a result of it. For example, by the end of these meetings one person decided to stop responding to the 'games' she felt

were being played by the service user and decided that she would learn to say no sometimes, to release herself from 24-hour caring, and to look after herself more.

This narrative from an experienced practitioner is a reminder that social workers who undertake assessments of older people and those with disabilities or illness need the skills of listening and attending to the grief and other psychological reactions of people to loss, death, dying, dementia, separation from partners and children. The fears which accompany the onset of dependency on others or becoming a carer need to be understood.

Assessment in criminal justice settings

The context of probation assessments and interviewing has changed radically over the past decade, although the major assessment tasks remain those of providing information for courts to assist sentencing, the supervision of offenders in the community and assessment about the risks posed to others by offenders on licence.

Assessments for courts

Historically, social inquiry reports have provided courts with social background information focused on the offender and their needs. Recommendations for 'alternatives to custody' would then be made, which the court might decide to implement. Since the implementation of the Criminal Justice Act 1991 and the subsequent amendments (National Standards 1995), pre-sentence reports provide courts with:

- offence analysis (including motivation, culpability, impact on victim and offender awareness of victim perspective);
- relevant information about offending, i.e. understanding offending and the best means of tackling it;

- assessment of risk of harm to the public, i.e. likelihood of further offences and level of risk of harm they would pose, along with the offender's motivation to change and the availability of measures to effect this change;
- a proposal as to the most suitable sentence, commensurate with the seriousness of the offence, which is most likely to reduce further offending.

Assessment for intervention

Historically, it was recognized that some needs are strongly linked to offending: for example, mental disorder, drugs or alcohol use, unemployment. There was a focus on meeting the offender's needs, with a view to diminishing the offending. There was some development of work directly focused on the patterns of thought and decision making that lead to offending behaviour, but this was fragmented and inconsistent.

Recent practice developments focus on 'what works'. This is direct intervention in offending behaviour patterns, backed up by secondary needs-based provision which is increasingly met through partnership organizations (McGuire 1995). Assessment at the report stage is also assessment for intervention. The proposal to the court, if for a community supervision order (Probation or Combination Order), incorporates the plan of work to be undertaken. The undercurrent of these developments is an increasing emphasis on assessing and managing risk to protect the public from harm (Home Office 1997; Kemshall and Pritchard 1996). There is a similar trend in child, family and adult services social work.

Implications for the use of counselling and interviewing skills in practice

Practitioners have questioned the relevance of social work approaches to the redefined criminal justice task. Is it still social work? Does a social work approach to interviewing still apply? What are the implications for practice?

It can be argued that there is nothing new here, except a shift in focus. Protection and control are not new to the probation agenda, nor are they exclusive to the agency. Child protection workers and approved mental health social workers grapple with similar issues. It may be that the explicit element of punishment sits less comfortably with a social work ethos, but it is more a matter of this now being explicit rather than masked in the probation role. It could be argued that this clarity is helpful in enabling the worker to be fully open about his or her authority and power.

Assessment therefore needs to take into account motivation and contributory factors to offending, the type and level of risk posed, motivation and capacity to change and suitability for particular approaches. Assessment interviews need to be highly focused, and require the challenging and testing of the offender's beliefs and attitudes. They incorporate a high level of motivational interviewing (Millar and Rollnick 1991). Information is sought about risk which could lead to the worker's actions being seen by offenders as not in their own perceived best interests, as, for example, in provisions for extended supervision post-sentence for a serious violent or sex offence (section 44, Criminal Justice Act 1991; section 58, Crime and Disorder Act 1998).

None of this, however, indicates a shift of technique, but a shift of purpose. *Listening, reflecting, open and focusing questions, confronting, summarizing* and *exploring options* remain relevant tools for practice. Nor does it necessarily present a fundamental shift from a humanistic/holistic approach. A wide view of the offender's situation is needed to help to establish the significant elements in their offending and how best to address them. The 'what works' paradigm recognizes that there are many layers to offending. It does not preclude meeting criminogenic and social welfare needs, but is a means of targeting scarce probation service resources to specific offence interventions, and then working in partnerships and through community resources to meet these other layers of need (McGuire 1995; Home Office 1998).

Victim perspective and risk management are about emphasizing the offender's social responsibilities. To enable the offender to take this on board the worker needs to offer more than simplistic information, but instead should provide a space for *reflective process* and *challenge*, which enable the offender to develop awareness and motivation to change. *Confrontation* and *challenge* are key skills in this work.

Can counselling skills be used in the service of punishment? This may seem a difficult area, but the focus on this dimension in criminal justice settings highlights the ethical dimensions of the uses of any skill or technique. It is vital to be open and explicit about the framework of statutory requirements and responsibility in which the interviewing takes place. Empowerment is not impossible. It is a matter of being clear about boundaries and accountabilities; about the scope and limitation of choice and options; and about a value base which takes into account disadvantage and discrimination when seeking explanations for people's offending behaviour as well as the means to engage them in reducing it in future (Williams 1996).

Practice example

Practitioners endeavour to use their skills to help their clients and to meet agency requirements. In this example a practitioner is able to demonstrate counselling skills in a criminal justice setting. First the client is assessed and then a programme of work is planned and undertaken.

Geoff was about to be sentenced for an offence of taking a car without the owner's consent. The initial interview for the pre-sentence report used *listening skills* and *focused questions* because of the need to obtain precise and accurate information. The worker wished to assess Geoff's awareness of his actions and his motivation to change. She used *open and closed questions* and *challenging* to test his view of the offence. As an outcome, and in line with procedural guidelines, she was able to recommend a Probation Order to the court. This proposal was considered suitable by the magistrates and the order was made.

A programme of work was planned for Geoff, together with his co-defendant Robert, who was also now on probation. It was planned with the agency objective in mind, which was to reduce the risk to the public of these two men repeating their offending. A cognitive approach was chosen because research has demonstrated that this can produce motivational, attitudinal and behavioural change in offenders. The first session of work was planned, with a series of *progressive questions* designed to approach specific aspects of the offending behaviour where change was sought. This was intended as a *focusing* method, with the *responses* to each question *reflected back* and *clarified* before the next one was asked. *Summaries* were to be used to draw the participants into contemplating their attitudes, behaviours and the impact car theft had on others. The worker planned to expect an amount of *silence*. Previous experience in a counselling context had demonstrated to her how this enables clients to collect their thoughts and/or contemplate new ideas and information. The practitioner trusted the idea that *allowing spaces and pauses* was a useful part of her repertoire of skills for asking offenders to consider their actions and motivations and the impact these had on others. Thus an intensive short programme of work used counselling skills to underpin a focused and cognitive approach to *challenging* the clients to change and plan a different future lifestyle.

Conclusion

Assessment and planning in all social work practice requires practitioners who are able to use their interpersonal skills in complex and sensitive work in a way which serves legislation and public policy. Assessment frameworks alone are only tools to collect information. They cannot balance, weigh risk and formulate plans. This task requires a reflective practitioner whose personal skills include the ability to engage with users to assess their motivation and capacity to change. This requires understanding of defensiveness, blocks and resistance, and the ability to enable users to abandon such strategies and engage openly in tasks. It requires the balance of personal and structural factors and being able to plan relevantly. It requires sustaining a relationship of partnership, often in difficult and unpromising circumstances. Professional judgement based on knowledge and skill is required in at least equal measure to well researched assessment tools. Advanced counselling skills are part of this professional skill.

Chapter 5

To intervene and provide services: relevant counselling skills

Assessment and planning in social work lead to referral to another agency or intervention and the provision of services. Qualifying social workers are expected to be able to:

> Intervene and provide services to achieve change through provision or purchase of appropriate levels of support care protection and control.
>
> (CCETSW 1995)

To intervene can mean to:

- broker;
- interfere in, prevent or modify the course of events;
- be situated between things;
- act in an extraneous way.

Intervention in social work encapsulates some of these meanings. Social workers intervene when they are negotiating and brokering between parties or acting directly to affect the life of a service user. The do-gooder, interfering image of social work which some people hold is based on fears and concerns about some highly publicized interventions: for example, where the legal powers of social workers have been used or withheld with perceived adverse outcomes.

To provide can mean to:

- equip someone with necessities;
- supply provisions.

Social workers offer services in kind. This providing aspect of social work intervention derives from its philanthropic origins, and the close link between statutory functions and welfare provision in legislation and policy. Examples are payments to maintain children, payments to assist offenders or direct provision of home care to older people. There are tensions in social work between care and control, providing and rationing, facilitating change and coercing. At assessment the social worker sifts and weighs how to intervene and provide in a way which is congruent with ethics, resources, legislation, procedural guidelines and social work values.

A group of trainee practitioners, asked to draw up a list of interventions, provided a complex and diverse response which included:

- *Methods*: assessment, care management, advocacy, counselling, advice giving, groupwork.
- *Tasks*: pre-sentence reports, benefits advice, hostel work, liaison work, legal action, supervision of court orders, referral.
- *Service provision*: placement provision (in residential homes, daycare, fostercare, respite care), childcare provision, day nursery places, advice about child-minding, education packages.

This list is not exhaustive, but it shows that social work intervention is wide ranging. In large bureaucratic organizations the emphasis is on commissioning services. Workers have to become skilled in handling this powerful role and acknowledge that one task is to ensure that the most suitable people receive the scarce resources available. In smaller agencies workers often intervene directly themselves.

Social work interventions can include:

- the use of social work theories and methods to plan interventions to achieve change;
- the use of the practitioner's personal skills in intervention;

- referral to provider agencies;
- purchase of services from provider agencies;
- direct provision of services in cash or kind;
- advocacy action to obtain service from another agency.

Most interventions contain these elements in combination. Counselling skills have their place, used in conjunction with theory and method to achieve change. The practitioner's counselling skills are significant in influencing the way services are delivered. This chapter considers the use of counselling skills in relation to theories, methods and the use of self in intervention. Worker style can make a fundamental difference to the way intervention and provision are made and evaluated by the service user.

Social work theories for intervention

All social work is underpinned by theory: 'to practice without theory is to sail an uncharted sea; theory without practice is not to sail at all' (Susser, quoted in Hardiker and Barker 1991: 87). Theoretical approaches are derived from a knowledge base which may be multi-faceted. They suggest that social work:

> requires a breadth of discipline knowledge (e.g. law, psychiatry and philosophy). Furthermore, social workers need to be sufficiently familiar with them to make informed choices, keep up to date with advances and to discard redundant theories.
>
> (Hardiker and Barker 1991: 87)

There follows a consideration of the underpinning psychological theories for intervention in social work practice, and some of the methods that derive from them, including a consideration of counselling skills in action through practice examples.

An eclectic approach to theory

To fulfil their tasks, social workers have drawn from other disciplines, including sociology (to understand the social construction of problems in society), psychology (to understand individual and group functioning) and social policy (to understand the structural factors which affect individuals). It can be argued that social work has been unnecessarily apologetic about this, because the strength of social work's eclectic history has made for versatile responses to the requirement to operate in diverse legal and bureaucratic frameworks. The advantages of the thoughtful eclectic approach are:

- the merging of theories for the benefit of the user, thus meeting individual need;
- avoidance of the narrow dogmatism which can accompany a single theory approach;
- the ability to be flexible and adapt to changing social policy and social conditions;
- the ability to work with other professionals from overlapping theory bases.

No new grand theories have emerged to underpin social work practice in the past two decades, but the application of theory in practice has been modified. Those approaches which are commonly recognized in the core texts for practice (Howe 1987; Compton and Galaway 1989; Coulshed 1991; Lishman 1991; Payne 1992) have been subject to redefinition and re-evaluation as social attitudes, values and beliefs change. They have particularly been re-examined for usefulness in relation to changes in legislation and policy which guide practice (Children Act 1989, NHS and Community Care Act 1990, Criminal Justice Act 1991). Social workers have proved resilient in adapting their tried methods to new legislative expectations (Hardiker and Barker 1994, 1996; Marsh and Triseliotis 1996b).

Three key approaches

With the context for an eclectic approach to theory having been set, there are some key psychological theories that deserve closer attention. There follows a brief summary of each key theory.

Psychodynamic theory

Psychodynamic practice was integrated into social work in Britain from the USA and became established in the 1950s, 1960s and 1970s (Brearley 1991). The ideas it espouses, about how personality is formed and developed, derive from Freudian psychoanalysis. Social work utilizes psychodynamic insights for: ways of understanding relationships, such as self and significant others; the link between past and present; and inner and outer experience. It is sometimes wrongly confused with the psychosocial approach. The psychosocial model derives concepts from psychodynamic theory and ego psychology, but combines the personal, social and practical into a more holistic framework (i.e. social casework). A narrow psychodynamic approach as practised in some counselling settings considers the external world only from the client's view. It is only rarely that such a narrow psychodynamic approach is used by social workers, but it has been highly influential in providing them with ways of understanding people. Furthermore, the important idea of the use of the relationship as an agent of change, which permeates social work practice, is essentially a psychodynamic one.

Psychodynamic ideas are particularly relevant in social work because of their influence in studies of human development (Fairbairn 1952; Erikson 1965; Winnicott 1960; Bowlby 1988; Rutter *et al.* 1994; Jacobs 1998). The place of psychodynamic thinking in social work is explored in a number of texts (Yelloly 1980; Pearson *et al.* 1988; Brearley 1991). At a very fundamental level it underpins both past and current research and practice in relation to children, families, older people and mental health. Psychodynamic ideas have also been applied in the literature on professional supervision (Kadushin 1997; Hawkins and Shohet 1989).

Learning theory

Behavioural social work, behavioural therapy and behaviour modification derive from learning theory. 'Learning theories form a body of theory about how behaviour changes as a result of experience, how behaviour is learned, maintained and unlearned'

(Hudson 1991: 123). Learning theory is based on scientific experiment and is consistently modified on the basis of new findings. Its origins come from classical experiments on animals, such as the work by Pavlov and Skinner, and work with children by Watson and Rayner (all described in some detail by Hudson 1991).

Behavioural social work begins with an assessment to establish a baseline from which to plan goals for change. Behaviours are analysed, and intervention techniques are based on operant learning and respondent conditioning. Social learning methods are then used as the tools for intervention. Evaluation of outcome is made against the initial baseline. There are full discussions in several key texts (Sheldon 1982; Hudson and MacDonald 1986; Howe 1987; Coulshed 1991; Payne 1992). Hudson and MacDonald (1986) outline a range of possible applications, including: anger control and child management with parents who abuse; helping foster carers to manage children's behaviour; work with adults in day centres and social skills training. Behavioural interventions are undertaken in psychiatric units to address obsessional behaviours and other issues of personal functioning.

Eco-systems theory

The ecological perspective is well established in the social sciences (Siporin 1975; Maluccio 1981; Garbarino 1982). It has emerged as the most comprehensive unifying framework, drawing from ethology, ecological psychology and ethnology. The framework presented is based on a cluster of key ideas:

- the person–environment relationship is continuous;
- person, behaviour and environment are mutually interdependent;
- systems theory is useful to analyse the ecology of the person in the situation;
- behaviour is site-specific;
- assessment and evaluation are through direct observation of the person–environment system;
- behaviour is the outcome of transactions between the person and the environment;
- behavioural science should seek to understand and analyse these interactions (Allen-Meares and Lane 1987).

The ecological approach takes a holistic view of the person in his or her environment and has the capacity for embracing other approaches. Assessment therefore gathers data giving equal emphasis to person and environment. The fact that data are drawn in relation to all variables makes the intervention and provision of services holistic.

These three key approaches, coupled with service provision and advocacy, are frequently the basis for intervention in social work practice. However, all three theoretical approaches rely heavily on the ability of the practitioner to make them operative through the use of interpersonal skills. Further, if an empowerment ideology is to underpin practice, the practitioner must be able to communicate theoretical understandings to the person with whom he or she is working, and achieve meaningful consent to process.

Practice example

This example shows the value of counselling skills, alongside other modes of helping. These are giving advice, providing information, direct action, teaching and systems change. There are psychodynamic, behavioural and ecological understandings informing the work.

David (21) lived at home with his mother and father. He had no specific diagnosed impairment, although he attended school for children with moderate learning difficulties until 16. He later transferred to a severe learning difficulties school. It was not apparent that he had a disability until he did not learn to speak. His first two years seemed relatively normal. Subsequently, his behaviour became hard to manage and his mother found it more and more difficult to cope. She felt intensely attached to him and this seemed allied to a hope that he did not have a disability. Little help was forthcoming, in practical terms or counselling, until he was 16, when he was excluded from a special needs further education course. Formal counselling proved to be a small but important part of the work with this family, although the use of counselling skills underpinned all the strategies used.

This family was not receiving all the welfare benefits to which there was a clear entitlement. Initially, David's mother Pat felt she had no right to such benefits, partly because of the years in which she had coped unaided. However, a successful claim opened her up to accepting the extent of her son's special needs and demonstrated her right to help. Information on services, behaviour management and parent groups was vital in breaking down isolation and helped to prioritize family needs. For example, the immediate problem was the absence of suitable daytime activities for David. A range of options was looked at and a further school placement identified. Pat continued to be very anxious, but over time this diminished as she began to trust the people working with David. A cognitive approach was useful here, which addressed and validated the feelings and experiences she had. For example, the worker acknowledged that the way teachers had treated David in the past was unhelpful, but enabled Pat to think that it could be different in future.

The setting up of a local parents' and carers' group introduced Pat to other people coping in similar circumstances, enabling her to share her feelings and concerns. This group could be seen in terms of systems change, as it recognized that many people in the locality were undergoing similar pressures which could be addressed in a group setting. Members themselves chose to use the group as a social support system rather than a campaigning body, and this choice too was important.

More formal counselling was introduced quite late in the social work intervention with David's family. Pat had identified that David was now more settled, the pressures on her had eased and the family had access to adequate support systems. However, she was diagnosed with nervous asthma and sometimes felt anxious and depressed. Her mother, with whom she had a difficult and strained relationship, had recently died. Individual counselling might help to get to the root of her anxiety.

A psychodynamic approach enabled her to examine her childhood, marriage and life since David had been born. She described the process as like opening a secret and frightening box and then being able to sort through it, keeping or discarding whatever she wanted. A particular issue was guilt about a brief extramarital affair she had many years ago. A more cognitive approach enabled Pat to absolve herself of the gnawing guilt when the affair was placed in the context of her lonely struggle to parent a child she loved but with whom it was so difficult to cope. After only three sessions, Pat's asthma was much improved and she had a more balanced overall perspective on her life. Much work was done in a short time because counsellor and client were well acquainted and trust was already established.

The worker's experience in the field of learning difficulties has shown her that formal counselling had a useful role to play, but only alongside adequate practical support systems. The use of counselling skills such as *giving undivided time, listening attentively* and *being non-judgemental, warm and accepting* is paramount at all stages of working with parents with a son or daughter with learning difficulties, from the initial diagnosis through to leaving home and afterwards. Regular support to alleviate isolation needs to be coupled with practical assistance, specialist knowledge of the child's condition, contact with other people in similar situations, coordination with other agencies, such as health and education, and planning for the future. Although not every family needs help all the time, there needs to be a recognition that easy access to a known, skilled, professional helper is there when needed. Parents benefit from routine support and the prevention of crisis, rather than response to crisis alone.

The worker commented:

> From a heavily psychodynamic casework approach of the 1950s we have come to the service-oriented approach of the 1990s, typified by assessment and care management procedures, enshrined in the NHS and Community Care Act 1990. Neither one nor the other is particularly useful in isolation, but both types of approach, offered to parents from the earliest stage possible, can enable families to help their learning disabled children to develop in a

more rounded, healthy and positive way to achieve more of their potential.

The same worker showed the use of a similar combination of approaches with another parent. In this case, issues around separation affected both parent and child. Jane, a single parent with an eight-year-old boy who had severe learning difficulties and behavioural problems, had not had an unbroken night of sleep since his birth.

> It was straightforward to set up a behavioural programme to work on this, but after a successful start this stuck at the point where he would go to bed, stay there and go to sleep, but only as long as his mother was still in the room with him. Jane seemed unable to take the next step and sit outside the room. By talking about and working on her feelings towards him she was able to see him less as a vulnerable, dependent baby and more as a growing child who could become more independent from her. Following this change of perspective Alexander coped better with going to sleep alone. Shortly after this, Jane moved out of her parent's home for the first time (she was in her 30s). This indicated the working out of some issues about her own separation from her parents, though this was not addressed directly in the counselling.

These accounts show how both psychodynamic and cognitive behavioural understandings informed the worker's interventions and can be used to provide services which were empowering and in line with legislative thinking. The worker's continued attention to ecosystems, in terms of environment, shows that a truly combined theoretical approach can be mobilized in the interests of families.

Social work methods

I wish to consider two examples of identified social work methods that have drawn on the main theories. They demonstrate how theory can be integrated with practice through usage. Workers can use methodology to fit the needs of users, rather than make users fit theories. Both these methods require underpinning counselling skills to make them effective.

Crisis intervention

Crisis intervention is based on psychodynamic theory and arose from attempts to provide a focused, brief form of therapy. The 'brief therapy' concept adds a cognitive element and matches social workers' aspirations to focus their own work more precisely. It was adopted in social work literature from the 1960s (Caplan 1964; Pittman 1966; Golan 1981).

People who seek social work attention are often in a state of distress. Whether this can be defined as a crisis is debatable, according to O'Hagan. Others, such as Caplan (1964), describe a 'crisis' as a temporary period of upset and disequilibrium, sometimes provoked by a transition or a traumatic event, where the person's usual abilities to manage are temporarily immobilized. It is the person's perception of events which defines crisis. Writers such as Golan (1981) and Roberts and Nee (1970) describe a crisis as having identifiable phases:

* the precipitating event and perception;
* the upset;
* inability to use previously tried coping methods and disequilibrium;
* the potential for hope;
* the intervention, which links current difficulties to past coping strategies;
* resolution or homeostasis restored within a few weeks (four to six).

Practice example
This example shows a worker undertaking crisis intervention using counselling skills to facilitate her approach. The setting is a children and families team, but a major focus of the work is the mental health of the adult carer for the children.

Penny (43) had three children, aged eleven, nine and five. Her husband died from cancer when the youngest was one. Since then she had suffered from episodes of severe mental ill-health which from time to time resulted in self-harm. A crisis occurred when Penny threatened to take an overdose and 'take them with me'. Social workers intervened and the children's names were placed on the child protection register because of the perceived risk of physical harm. There were mixed feelings among the staff about this because Penny had never hit or threatened her children, yet clearly there was a risk. The registration resulted in Penny becoming angry and hostile towards social services. The allocated social worker had misgivings about the registration and about the monitoring role which she had to undertake. However, counselling skills 'saw me through'.

Attention was offered through *actively listening*. *Empathy* was employed to assess Penny's concerns. Most crucially, *non-critical acceptance* was shown because Penny had very low self-esteem, which could be exacerbated by the monitoring. Penny then revealed that she was sexually abused in childhood by her grandfather. She had never been able to discuss this with any of the therapeutic helpers she had known over a period of five years. Her husband had been her main support and his loss had triggered severe depression.

The new worker persisted in the supportive/ monitoring role, utilizing counselling skills throughout, while remaining clear about the child protection worker's role and open about Penny's view of the intervention. At the same time, the worker made it clear she was not going away and cared about Penny's progress as a person and parent. After a few weeks the situation stabilized, and after six months deregistration was recommended. Despite a further episode of self-harm, the verbal threats to the children ceased. It was considered appropriate to build on the practitioner's work, and a specialist child and family counsellor became involved.

Penny had changed her outlook and accepted some responsibility for the effect of her actions on her

children. She began to develop a better relationship with
her psychiatrist. After 12 months the case was closed,
leaving the children and family counsellor involved
and some supportive mental health provision in place.
Penny's reaction to the practitioner's final visit affirmed
that she had valued the supportive approach combined
with the monitoring functions. She even asked if she
could get in touch if she needed to. She paid close
attention to the worker's affirmation of the progress
she had made during the work they had experienced
together.

The worker felt strongly that it was the relationship
built on counselling skills that made progress possible,
despite the authoritarian monitoring that was her legal
duty. The improvements for the mother and children
were indications of a good outcome. It is possible to
intervene in a decisive and authoritative way to meet
legal duties and still offer support. In this intervention
it was the therapeutic abilities of the practitioner that
largely contributed to the progress achieved.

Task-centred practice

Task-centred social work is a framework for practice, developed
within social work from ego psychology and the use of contract.
It is a focused way of supporting clients to resolve identified
areas in their lives which are difficult. The origins of the method
can be found in American literature in the 1960s and 1970s
(Reid 1963; Reid and Epstein 1972, 1976). Task-centred work
became established in social work to avoid unfocused long-term
interventions which encouraged unnecessary dependency. Reid
and Shyne (1969) suggested that brief work could produce as good
results as long-term intervention. The task-centred approach can
be seen as applicable to a problem solving framework requiring:

- client agreement;
- an open agenda about client and worker activities;
- specificity about concrete goals and tasks;
- allocation of tasks;

- time limits;
- review and evaluation;
- reciprocal accountability (both worker and client taking responsibility for outcomes).

It is important that the tasks selected are achievable and structured.

Practice example

The following narrative describes a worker using a task-centred approach with a young man with a serious mental health difficulty. The achievement of the task-centred goals is dependent upon good communication and counselling skills.

Mikesh (39) was referred to a hostel by field social workers. He found living alone in the community impossible. He had no social or recreational life, was depressed, drinking and frequently admitted to hospital. The hostel stay was to help him to start structuring his time, becoming involved with people, reducing his alcohol intake, sorting out his previous accommodation and debts and moving back into the community on a better basis. He was out of touch with his relatives as a result of his drinking patterns. At the time of his admission he was too depressed to consider living alone.

The relationship building phase began with the allocated keyworker using *listening skills* and *reflecting back*. There was no attempt to ask questions or delve into his background (there was enough on file already). Instead, the practitioner worked to understand the client's view of his present situation. Mikesh told his own story: depression, anger and frustration built up to a point where drinking got him through the day. He had not worked since his schizophrenia diagnosis. He had few friends. His hope was that the hostel would somehow 'get him out of the rut' and give him some confidence to have a better life.

The worker *listened* carefully and encouraged Mikesh to tell his story. He used *empathy* to think himself into Mikesh's position and to formulate a supported way forward. His conclusion was that Mikesh believed himself powerless to do anything to change his isolation. He *checked this interpretation* of powerlessness with Mikesh by *summarizing and paraphrasing* Mikesh's own words, but adding the term powerlessness. Mikesh said he could not see things getting better. There seemed no point in anything. Everything he had tried failed. In any case, if he was so sick what was the point? This lack of motivation clarified how no amount of encouragement to do things had helped, especially as his illness contributed to his self-perception. The worker now had to find a way to support and enable without controlling or pushing the client into activity which he found pointless.

At the next session the worker *explored the way the client experienced problems*. Mikesh said he panicked and felt overwhelmed. The worker offered to facilitate and support work with Mikesh, if he could just list what panicked him. The list referred to: the mess his flat was in; the rent, water, gas and electric arrears; anxiety that the courses and voluntary work offered were too much for him; fears of leaving the hostel.

Mikesh said he felt better for having said all of this. They made a verbal agreement to work together on one thing at a time. With the worker using *listening skills*, *accurate responding* and *empathy*, they had reached a viable plan. An agreed period of four months was allocated to begin some work. This began with a visit to the flat, giving up the tenancy, making arrangements to settle bills and planning for a future tenancy. This eased some pressure. Meanwhile, some drink reduction work was undertaken and Mikesh began to do some voluntary work in a community centre with Asian elders. The worker felt a good start had been made.

The practitioner's use of self in intervention

The positive or negative valuations placed on social work interventions by service users often concern the practitioner's interpersonal style rather than the theories or methods espoused.

Service users may be primarily concerned with whether the practitioner was respectful in providing what was needed or helping with a difficulty. Interventions in social work are therefore about roles and tasks, agency function, theories and methods and the use of self in carrying these through. In a time of scarce or inappropriate resources, the personal manner and skills of the worker are highly significant in the process of intervention. The worker's presence and counselling, brokering and negotiating abilities might prove to be the significant factor in the effectiveness of the work.

Practice example

In this example, the worker had to intervene with no specialized resources immediately available. Zoe (15) was saying that her father had sexually abused her from the age of seven. Her mother became aware of this when the abuse had stopped, but the offences were not yet reported to the police.

Before she shared what had happened, Zoe had moved out of home to stay with some close friends of her parents. She remained there and they were approved as private foster parents. Her father was subsequently arrested and remanded on bail. Zoe's two sisters continued to live with her mother. Her father moved out. The practitioner identified several areas of intervention. These were: individual support to Zoe, her sister and her mother; support and assessment of the foster carers; relationship work between Zoe and her mother (feelings were running high); mediation work between the foster carers, the mother and Zoe.

The worker used counselling skills in personal work with Zoe. The first step was sitting with her in a park near the foster carers' home and *listening*. She ensured that this listening was very *attentive*, to try to understand what Zoe felt about what had happened to her. *Linking* was used to make sense of Zoe's experiences, to hold them together. After this, in more formal sessions, Zoe was asked to write her feelings on a shield with four parts. This exercise showed up how worthless she felt. At this point the practitioner focused verbal interventions on *reflecting back* and *summarizing* what Zoe said. This was important because sometimes Zoe became very upset and the reflection back of her feelings was supportive.

The process was explained to Zoe, and how the counselling approach was different from an ordinary conversation. This seemed to give Zoe the security that the practitioner was really trying to understand her. It was also important because her mother often reinterpreted and gave a completely different version of events, so it was vital to validate the client's own experiences. The client was subsequently referred to a therapeutic service but the worker felt able to support the people involved through a difficult time. Zoe was able to make good use of the specialized therapeutic help she was subsequently offered.

Social worker qualities

Social workers need a combination of qualities and skills in their intervening and providing activities. Compton and Galaway (1989) suggest six qualities of maturing people who experience themselves as living, growing and developing, unafraid of life and enjoying the process of living, with all the struggle this may involve. These are:

- creativity;
- intellectual openness;
- receptivity, holding most solutions to the problems of life as tentative;
- capacity to observe self;
- desire to help;
- courage.

They also identify six sets of essential elements: concern for others for their own sake; commitment and obligation; acceptance and expectation; empathy; authority and power; genuineness and congruence. This is in contrast to Keith-Lucas's (1972) list of people who are experienced as unhelpful. These are:

- those interested in knowing about people rather than in serving them;
- those impelled by strong personal needs to control, to feel superior, to be liked;
- those who have solved problems similar to the problems of people in need of help, but have forgotten what it cost them to do so;
- those primarily interested in retributive justice and moralizing.

Personal qualities, values and attitudes overlap with skills, but skills can be distinguished as the abilities or techniques which are used to communicate the essential values of respect and understanding. It is particularly important to demonstrate such skills when working with vulnerable and marginalized groups in society. Intervention and the provision of services are then underpinned by those aspirations for which the first competences have already provided a foundation: clear communication; the involvement of the client in partnership; empowerment approaches which enable and work on strengths while supporting vulnerabilities. Thus the personal qualities of the worker are applied through their skills.

Empathy

Empathy is important for intervening and providing services in a way which combines authority and understanding. Empathy is often mistakenly confused with sympathy (an outpouring of our own identification with the other, showing pity and concern in a way which perhaps fails to understand the other because it comes from our own concern). Empathy is a capacity for objective concern.

Empathy is often thought of as a personal quality. Many people do develop their capacity to enter another's world through their family interactions and experiences of life. There is evidence that the capacity for empathy is a positive predictor for parental ability to provide children with the love and nurture they need (Rosenstein 1995). The accurate empathy needed for social work practice is a skill, both built from the personal qualities with which each of us starts, and developed through supervised practice.

Empathy is the capacity to enter into the feelings and experiences of another; to understand what the other is experiencing as if you were the other; to be detached about your own self and identity in the process. There is an emotional content and an intellectual element to the skilled exercise of empathy.

Learning to be empathic requires knowledge (for example, examination of the stereotypes we may be carrying around about others, and the acquisition of cultural and structural understandings about society). It also requires the ability to feel with someone else, while observing the boundaries of what your own feeling is. This is particularly important with shared experiences. Workers' own experiences of loss might give some clues as to how others experience loss but, without the capacity for empathy, they might simply transfer their own experiences on to someone else whose reaction is quite different from their own.

Some bereaved people feel rage, others sadness, others regret. How grief is experienced depends on personality, previous experiences, religious outlook and the relationship with the deceased. Practitioners need to be aware of the range of normal responses which exist in any particular situation. It is suggested that in terminal illness some fight, some deny, some are angry and some despair. All these reactions are valid for the individuals concerned.

Empathic understanding enables workers to accept and enter the world of the client irrespective of their own personal and cultural baggage. This is important in intervening and providing services because, if the necessary step of entering another's world and involving him or her is not taken, intervention and provision are likely to be rejected or fail.

It is sometimes suggested that empathy implies agreement with, or support for, the other's actions, thoughts or feelings, and that it is difficult or wrong to empathize with people who have, for example, killed or abused someone. However, empathy is not sympathy or approval. In an important way it is value free; it does not prescribe or collude with actions. Empathy can be used with a client in assessing and planning for where he or she is. The practitioner is still free to be clear about society's or the agency's view of the client's values and actions.

Empathy identifies and works with difference constructively. It is a personal skill which can be refined and developed from the personal qualities of concern for others, to embrace a range of values. Empathizing involves the professional use of self in intervention in the lives of others. Fitting clients to services is ultimately a time-wasting and costly exercise. Workers' plans which undermine the user's wishes and needs usually break down. Empathy is the ability to see the world from clients' point of view, and to stay alongside them to plan appropriately.

Older people who find themselves needing services often have strong views about becoming dependent. For many previously active socially productive people the change of role profoundly affects their sense of self. Without an understanding of what this means for individuals, including understanding their background, culture, previous employment and lifestyle, it is easy to be well meaning and prescribe a raft of services which are rejected; and then to describe this reaction as uncooperative. It may be that fewer, more appropriate and agreed services are more effective. For example, the loss of social stimulation might be more important to one person than her inability to cook a hot meal. There is no point in offering domiciliary meals to someone who would like a day out, or group activity to someone who is happy with his own company but is tired of living on sandwiches. Neither meals nor daycare are of any use if they are offered in a way which takes no account of cultural preferences, vegetarian diets or client motivation regarding the service.

This may seem elementary, but sometimes the energy expended in labelling could be better spent taking time to intervene appropriately. The place of counselling skills here is listening and responding, so the service offered fits the needs of the consumer as far as possible. Such skills assist the practitioner to clarify roles, agree courses of action, use the appropriate working methods, support and sustain users through transition and change, negotiate packages of care and become involved in active evaluation.

Practice example

This example shows a worker using empathy to intervene and provide a service for a 14-year-old and her grandparents. It includes explicit use of social work theory and methods and counselling skills to underpin the interventions.

Gemma (14) was raised by her grandparents and still lived with them. Her mother lived nearby with her husband, his son from a previous relationship (12) and their two daughters (seven and five). The client, Gemma, had a boyfriend (Steve). Gemma was not attending school and the education department applied to court for a supervision order. The case was referred to social services for an assessment under section 47 of the Children Act 1989. Gemma was known to the department, as her grandparents had frequently asked for help. The referrals involved issues around involvement with older men and unlawful sexual intercourse. Usually support from social services had resulted in Gemma's return to school and reunification with her grandparents.

When the practitioner contacted Gemma she was not cooperative. She described the intervention of education and the police as punishing. She thought no one was concerned with her or what she wanted, only with school attendance (*active listening, minimal prompts*). The worker decided to engage the young woman in self-assessment, as she surmised (*empathy*) that loss of control over her life was an issue. Her initial approach (*avoiding questions*) and her use of an eco-map to gain information about the family and the impact of other agencies and individuals served to build a constructive relationship.

The worker's assessment was that a supervision order would alienate Gemma further, a view supported by the grandparents, who described Gemma as 'anti everything'. By building a relationship where the practitioner and client were working together to make sense of what was happening, the practitioner was in a position to recommend to the court work on a voluntary basis for six months. Use of counselling skills enabled the practitioner to achieve a working plan congruent with the principles of the Children Act 1989 (welfare of the child, parental partnership, avoidance of court orders, least intrusive intervention, incorporating the wishes and feelings of the young person).

The intervention which followed was a combination of counselling and active task-centred support. The areas the client identified for work were: issues about school; the grandparents' objection to her boyfriend; feelings about not being in her mother's new family and the circumstances around her birth and upbringing. Verbal task-centred agreements were made, facilitated by *listening, responding, clarifying* and *goal setting*. Careful *listening* to Gemma established that formal written plans had previously alienated her and made her feel that her wishes were discounted. This was *respected* throughout, and although necessary agency records were kept, written work was minimized. The worker carefully chose methods that were complementary and did not contradict each other at a theoretical level. Her task-centred practice was based on classic texts (Reid and Shyne 1969; Coulshed 1991; Payne 1992).

A counselling aim was adopted 'to give the client an opportunity to explore, discover and clarify ways of living more resourcefully and towards greater well-being' (British Association for Counselling 1984). Interventions were directed to the client's beliefs about herself, which guided her feelings and behaviour. Her perception of being misjudged about her boyfriend, by grandparents and professionals, conditioned her thoughts and actions. The worker's *acceptance* meant that Gemma talked for the first time about herself, leading into a phase of *exploration* of her view of her situation.

The practitioner now *confronted* and *challenged* her preconceived beliefs, while still accepting that Gemma's perception remained valid. This led to exploration about what might facilitate her return to school and about her place in her family. It emerged that Gemma believed she had nothing to contribute in school or the family, but that she felt valued with Steve. The practitioner stayed *person-centred* in this stage of the work, enabling Gemma to consider dimensions of her world for herself.

There were crises at various times, including threats from Steve towards the grandparents when Gemma decided to end her relationship with him. The police were called to ask him to leave the grandparents' home. Other work was done with school to facilitate her return, although the worker was as frustrated as the client was at times by slow responses from other agencies.

Opportunities were provided for Gemma to evaluate and plan her future with social workers, the education department and her grandparents. The person-centred approach had resulted in her being seen by others more as an individual and not just as a 'truant'.

This user-led approach, underpinned by counselling skills, created some changes in the client's self-perception and in the system with which she was in conflict. It was time-consuming but it met agency goals and avoided more intrusive and expensive interventions, such as court proceedings, supervision orders or accommodation.

Conclusion

Interventions in social work depend upon legislation, policy and procedural frameworks. They are informed by social work theories and methods. Material resources are offered and provided. The process is implemented and coordinated by an individual practitioner, whose abilities, judgements and choices uniquely affect the quality of the total service provision. A counselling skills approach to the interaction is consistent with the provision of an authoritative, ethical, holistic approach to a range of practice tasks and methods of work.

Chapter 6

To work in organizations: relevant counselling skills

Social workers need to understand the opportunities and constraints of the organizations where they work. This involves understanding the nature of organizations – formal, informal, bureaucratic, hierarchical (Smith 1991; Handy 1993) – and possessing appropriate personal skills to operate effectively within them. Qualifying social workers must be able to:

> Contribute to the work of the organisation.
>
> (CCETSW 1995)

This means: working as an accountable and effective member of the organization; contributing to the planning, monitoring and control of resources; contributing to the evaluation, effectiveness, efficiency and economy of services; being accountable for own behaviour and practice; working within policies and procedures; establishing and maintaining working relationships with team members and other agency staff; identifying and advising on changing and emerging demands on resources; seeking feedback from service users and relevant others about the effectiveness and appropriateness of the service provided; facilitating others to make suggestions about improvements to services; enabling service users and others to make representations, including complaints.

This relationship between the worker and employing agency is one in which it is essential to maintain the appropriate personal and professional boundaries. Counselling skills used within the organization are therefore subject to agency expectations and purposes. The role of the social work professional has been defined in the past through boundaries with other professions, such as law, medicine and teaching. Consequently, there has been a search for a distinctive social work role and a tendency to public and internal doubt about the legitimate professional territory of social work. There has also been debate about the knowledge, skills and value systems that equip social workers for their tasks.

Traditionally, social work brought personal and helping skills to other professional settings, such as hospitals and courts. The first social workers were in charity organizations. The work done by volunteers with prisoners, destitute children, the mentally ill, older and infirm adults was formalized into the welfare state during the twentieth century. The new professional social workers of the 1940s found roles in the penal system, children's services, education, mental health and hospital services, as well as retaining a substantial presence in charitable and voluntary sector caring services. The social work presence in some of the more controlling aspects of public welfare was an important contributor to keeping public services humane and caring. This reflected the contribution of religious and other philanthropic concerns in society, as well as the recognition in socialism that individual misfortune or deprivation is not simply about personal deficits, but also about the ways in which individual life experience is affected by structural social inequalities. Social workers were employed to humanize and mitigate the effects of state intervention in the lives of citizens. They quickly developed a role in challenging the inequalities they perceived in host organizations.

The reorganization of social workers into large bureaucratic social services departments in the 1970s clearly identified them as a discrete professional grouping. The old divisions between almoners, children's department workers and mental health department social workers were eroded as new generic services were created. This continued until local authority reorganization and a spate of legislation affecting social work tasks in the late 1980s and early 1990s meant that social workers were regrouped in specialist teams, while still employed in local authority social services departments.

This chapter considers the ways in which being part of an organization affects the professionalization of helping skills, as well as the concept of relatedness with the client. As Chapter 1 suggested, some social workers would say that counselling skills are not part of their work, and that the concept of relationship cannot be central to the tasks of modern social work. These assertions arise because of the nature of the structures within which social workers employed by the large bureaucracies operate, and the roles which these organizations delineate.

Human services organizations

Hasenfield (1983) analyses how bureaucratic service organizations are a product of the growth of the welfare state, designed to manage and promote the personal welfare of citizens, and establish mechanisms whereby eligibility for services is assessed, so that resources are shared out equitably. In order to do this, organizations use formal rules, procedures and systems of accountability. The core activities of these service organizations are 'relations between staff and clients'. Mechanisms are established that regulate issues of intake, who makes decisions about the activities and mandates of others and who has authority over resources. Within these large organizations, both clients and front-line workers may lack power, because the organization of the agency mediates the 'series of transactions by which resources and services are exchanged' (Hasenfield 1983: 178) and 'the power advantage of human service organizations enables them to exercise considerable control over the lives of recipients of their services' (Hasenfield 1983: 180).

The structure usually contains complaint mechanisms to challenge decisions, but these may seem so bureaucratic that workers lose confidence in their effectiveness. Informal networks of consensus between workers and clients may arise which subvert or sidestep formal procedures. Lipsky (1980) describes social workers in large public agencies as 'street-level bureaucrats', and writes:

> the decisions of street-level bureaucrats, the routines they establish, and the devices they invent to cope with uncertainties and work pressures, effectively become the public

policies they carry out. I argue that public policy is not best understood as made in the legislatures or top floor suites of high ranking administrators, because in important ways it is actually made in the crowded offices and daily encounters of street-level workers. I point out that policy conflict is not only expressed as the contention of interest groups but is also located in the struggles between individual workers and citizens who challenge or submit to client processing . . . At best street-level bureaucrats respond by inventing benign modes of mass processing that more or less permit them to deal with the public fairly appropriately and successfully, at worst they give in to favouritism, stereotyping and routinizing, all of which serve private or agency purposes.

(Lipsky 1980: x)

Lipsky (1980: 193) poses some important questions, which he then addresses, such as:

- Should teachers, police officers and welfare workers look for other work rather than perpetuate unfair, ineffective or destructive public practices?
- Should they carry on contributing to such practices?
- Should they struggle from within to change the conditions by which citizens are processed by agencies?
- How much can human intervention be eliminated from human service professions?

He concludes that 'the fact is we must have people making decisions and treating other people in the public services', and that these agencies can 'reinforce the relationships between citizens, both clients and workers, and the state. Many of the criticisms . . . focus on the extent to which people fail to receive appropriate, equitable or respectful encounters.'

Taking these criticisms as points of departure, three major lines of analysis are discussed:

- encouraging client autonomy and influence over policy;
- improving current street-level practice;
- helping street-level bureaucrats to become more effective proponents of change.

Good practices are described as clear communication, advocacy, guides to rights, summaries of transactions, routine reviews, investigation and accountability (Lipsky 1980: 185). Discretion is identified as another significant element that needs monitoring (Lipsky 1980: 196).

This analysis of the role of social workers in their organizations is important for us, because it contextualizes the arena in which counselling skills can be used. Counselling skills can be part of facilitating encounters within the bureaucracy, but care needs to be taken that this is ethical, and that counselling skills are not being used in the service of pacifying those who have been denied a legitimate request. It should instead broker entitlements, advocate and facilitate appeals or complaints as needed.

Social work territory

The boundary of social work territory and the nature of social work tasks are still being debated. Lhullier and Martin (1994) write about the unease social workers appear to have in their profession. They comment on the struggle to work against 'social exclusion' and the insecurity and isolation which workers may feel. Writing from a knowledge of the French system, they re-appraise the contract between society and the profession. The importance of multi-agency work, partnerships in social action, objectives of inclusion, avoidance of bureaucracy and improved professional training is highlighted. Their view of the path ahead is encouraging, affirming that 'perhaps the crisis in social work is only a new form of growing pains. Clearly social work continues on its path towards more effective professionalization' (Lhullier and Martin 1994: 364).

Abbott (1995), writing from an American perspective, produces an analysis which resonates with the situation in Britain. He documents how groups in society identified with social work have changed, particularly noting that 'probation is present but will gradually disappear' (Abbott 1995: 546). Three notions of social work as a profession are described – functional, ecological and networking – from which speculations about the future are made. He suggests that:

- social workers should not be disturbed about changing structures of professionalism, most professions undergo transition and change;
- social work, as a discipline of connections across boundaries, is related to changes in other professions;
- public assistance is an area where social work holds the territory;
- the public perception of social workers is still that 'they help people', and social work is unusual in having retained a public image based on a character trait.

He concludes that the environment looks in many ways as it did a hundred years ago:

> Again we have a welter of social services so confused that no one can figure it out. Again, the populations to be served are both difficult and despised. Again there is a diffuse sense that those institutions that ought to be caring for individual welfare in this society are failing in that task. It was from such a complex conjuncture that the old profession of social work emerged. It emerged through the drawing together of groups that represented particular sides of various debates over welfare. It was a coalition of diverse and diversely different groups, a 'social work of boundaries'. I think we are at a juncture where a new such coalition could emerge.
>
> (Abbott 1995: 562)

Counselling and relationship skills remain as a set of abilities which can assist social workers negotiate boundaries between individuals and welfare services in the interests of the public. Counselling skills are used to represent users accurately to managers, and vice versa, and to support individuals through turbulence and change. Counselling skills are used to negotiate the interface between social inclusion and exclusion.

Preoccupation with change is reflected in recent articles in *Community Care*. Sone (1996) considers the use of technology in commissioning services and some of the anxieties about change which this generates. The question is posed: 'Will social workers become form filling automatons?' The answer has to be 'no'. Technology speeds up recording and access to information about services and resources, but as Stout, chair of BASW, asserted when interviewed, 'social workers will never just sit in an office and fill in forms. They cannot make an assessment for a full care management package without social work intervention. They can't function without interacting with clients' (Sone 1996).

Literature is currently concerned with the possibility of new multidisciplinary alliances. Social workers may not always be employed in social services departments in local authorities, but may be working in new structures, in new coalitions with health, housing, education and juvenile justice. It would be useful if corporate agencies were organized in such a way as to be one-stop, accessible services responsive to local need and offering better service delivery. However, as Eaton (1998) writes, 'it comes down to the same thing; it is not the structure, but the staff and the attitude they and their managers have, that matter most.' The role of social work has recently been re-evaluated under pressure from the concepts of market, quality assurance and value for money which have permeated public services. The Probation Service, which employed a largely social work trained workforce, is reappraising the knowledge, values and skills needed for supervising offenders in both prisons and the community. This is reflected in the new qualifying training arrangements currently being implemented. It is hoped that social workers will work in organizations which allow individuals to respond humanely to service users in an accountably autonomous way characterized not only by technical rationality but also by reflection in action (Schon 1983), in which the use of counselling skills to facilitate practice will remain ethically viable.

Since 1979, government has been critical of the lack of efficiency and consumer choice in the public sector bureaucracies that arose from the welfare reforms of the 1940s and 1970s. The answer to this is constructed as a market approach, which provides a mixed economy of welfare services, with the local authorities as enablers and purchasers. This change of philosophy inevitably affects social workers at the interface with the public. It remains possible to maintain a relationship to consumers within practice, and to use counselling skills to facilitate choice without being manipulative.

Practice example

This example shows counselling skills used within the
framework of the community care assessment process
undertaken in a large bureaucracy. It is representative
of the nature of social work practice with older people
needing residential care. It is a typical 'routine' piece
of work, yet the needs of the people are personal
and acute.

Mrs Davis needed an emergency placement because
her husband and carer, Mr Davis, suffered a heart attack.
Mrs Davis was physically fragile and suffering from
dementia. A short-term emergency bed in a local
psychiatric unit was provided, but after Mr Davis was
discharged from hospital there were concerns about him
resuming her care. Mr Davis felt his main need was to be
with his wife. He was visited at home and his needs were
assessed. He was found to need minimal assistance with
personal tasks, but much assistance with domestic tasks
(lack of mobility, wheeziness and advice from the
hospital to relax because of his heart condition).
Mrs Davis had been assessed separately and the two
assessments identified different needs in terms of the
physical and mental aspects. It was clear that the
overriding concern was the couple's wish to be together.
Mr Davis could not relax when apart from Mrs Davis,
and she fretted for him.

A joint placement was sought, but it had to be one
that could meet Mrs Davis's mental health needs as well
as Mr Davis's physical care. This meant that when a
suitable establishment was identified, most residents
except Mr Davis had cognitive impairment. The couple
moved into a shared room, on a trial basis, with a four-
weekly review arranged. Mr Davis, however, began to
find the demands of his wife and living with so many
confused people very tiring. None the less, he felt that
he would miss his wife if he returned home. He was also
worried about losing his accommodation. It was agreed
that he would stay the month on a trial basis. He would
have a separate room and the staff would link him to
some of the less confused residents so that he had some

social support within the establishment. The social worker would visit him weekly.

These visits were important, as they gave Mr Davis the opportunity to share his concerns with someone he could trust. The practitioner *listened* to his comments about the establishment, which were *fed back* to staff for action, especially as introductions to less confused residents were not made. The limitations of the placement were talked through and Mr Davis was able to reflect on what he would say at the forthcoming review. He shared concerns about the future, worry that relatives were not visiting and some of his feelings about Mrs Davis (*attentive listening, exploratory questions, clarifying, summaries, ventilation of feelings, empathy*). There were also practical issues, such as making a will and sorting out financial arrangements. Unfortunately, Mr Davis suffered a further heart attack and returned to hospital just before the review date.

This snapshot of intervention, typical of work with older couples, shows social workers competently completing their legally mandated assessments, enabling the purchase of appropriate care and reviewing progress. However, within that procedural framework, the practitioner had built a relationship with Mr Davis, and other significant work could be achieved. The worker used counselling skills in an enabling way to help him to express his views and exercise his choice as much as budgetary restraints allowed.

Initially, he said that his emotional need to be with his wife was more important to him than any needs regarding his physical disabilities. When worry about her was beginning to affect him, counselling skills were used to help him to talk about the unavoidable changes in circumstances. He had, in a very short time, to cope with his partner's increased confusion, his own inability to go on caring for her, worries about moving out of his home and worries about his own deteriorating physical health. He wanted to care for his wife as long as needed, but her relatively good physical health compared with his own ill-health was changing this. He talked to his social worker about his concerns about his own death, and the fact that he could no longer talk with his wife, who had always been there for him. He talked about the absence of solutions and various family concerns. In retrospect, the worker wished they had been able to talk more about his concerns about dying before Mrs Davis, because Mr Davis died following the second heart attack and hospital admission.

The practitioner's work was based on Scrutton (1989), who writes that, 'at its simplest, counselling is no more and no less than the development of a warm, empathetic and understanding relationship with those who are experiencing emotional and social stress, giving them time, listening to their troubles amd responding to them with sympathy' (Scrutton 1989: 6–7).

In the weekly sessions in the time between assessment and review, the practitioner made good use of personal skills in the service of effective social work practice. The worker reflected that *unconditional positive regard, empathic understanding* and *genuineness* were offered, but that *empathic understanding* did not mean denying problems. Perhaps opportunities to open up difficult subjects and *allow the expression of fears and worries* were not taken enough. At times the social work role meant giving advice about what might be most useful. However, within the limits of the social work role it was possible to *listen* to Mr Davis's wishes. The worker could *attend to feelings about the loss* of social role, friends, home and a lifelong companion through a degenerative illness.

Such skills can be used to facilitate even limited choices. An entirely administrative approach to the social work task would have been disempowering and potentially ageist. Older service users face a substantial loss of status and identity as illness and disability affect their usual coping methods. This is compounded by the illness and death of peers and partners and the realization of the nearness of their own death. As these limitations increase, the worker's respect for their ability to exercise as much control as possible is crucial. A positive choice can be made to practise in a person-centred way within bureaucratic procedures.

Voluntary sector agencies

So far this chapter has been concerned with publicly maintained practice in large bureaucracies. However, these are not the only providers of social work services. Voluntary, charitable and private organizations are crucially important as employers of qualified social workers, trainers of social workers and providers of direct services to the public. Examples are: Barnado's, The Children's Society and the NSPCC in children's services; MIND, MENCAP and Age Concern in adult services. Social workers are employed in some housing services, alcohol and drugs advisory services, family centres, residential care services for children and adults, advice centres and advocacy services.

Many of these agencies offer therapeutic services which require a high level of counselling skills, and engage in direct counselling work. It is therefore important to have the personal skills to work in large and small organizations in an accountable and effective way. Smaller organizations, or those with less hierarchical structures, give practitioners the opportunity for different kinds of practice. For example, the Family Service Unit, a large national organization, is characterized by small units that operate at local level, responding to local need, enabling a variety of practice, including community work, group work and intensive individual family support, and using therapeutic techniques based on counselling approaches. There is evidence that consumers respond well to accessible, informal mechanisms for helping. These give workers scope for creativity in their methods and interventions. Family centres show how this kind of organizational approach works.

Practice example
A social worker based in a family centre, with open access to parents, was able to offer counselling, based on feminist approaches and a cognitive model, to a young parent, in a way that would not have been possible in a social services department. The woman, Louise, requested

individual counselling because of her depression. The centre's open door policy made this possible and she was offered counselling through a structured weekly meeting. The outcome was a positive one. When the work was complete, Louise said that she felt able to separate out her problems and to recognize the issues she needed to work on. She had begun to see that meeting her own needs was equally important to meeting her family's needs; that although she still felt unhappy at times, she realized that this was in part due to the way she had been treated in the past. The practitioner concluded, 'for my part, what Louise told me made me realize our counselling had achieved some positive purpose.'

Another example was given in Community Care (23 July 1997). A family were working with social services following the sexual abuse of a child by a relative. After monitoring and case conferences, some specified work was recommended in relation to family dynamics and the child's behaviour. The mother wrote:

> We asked if the work could be done at the family centre, not only because of the friendliness of the place but because we had built up a relationship with the staff there.
>
> We will be co-operating fully with the family centre to do this work, so we will not have to go back to the case conference. We do realise how silly we were not to admit to the injury to Kieran straight away, but we panicked, thinking the children would be taken away from us.
>
> Looking back we have received a lot of support and help from the family centre, not just with the children, but also with our marriage. We do acknowledge that social workers do not always have the time to do the long term work with families that family centres can.

If children and families are to work in partnership with social workers, this can only truly occur when the choices made by users are on the basis not of coercion, but recognizing need and genuinely cooperating. A climate of trust facilitates this. Fear leads to covering up and avoidance. The family strengths approach to working with families is well documented (Whalley 1994; Scott and O'Neill 1996), and uses an empowering approach based on relationship skills, without losing focus or authority.

Inter-agency work

Social workers need counselling skills to work in their own organizations and also for effective inter-agency work. Many of the 'failures' of childcare and adult mental health services have been due to ineffective inter-agency communication. Verbal interactions of a high quality are necessary. Careful listening about what is available from another organization, careful checking and responding, the ability to question and challenge and the ability to make a considered and boundaried set of effective working professional relationships are all vital.

The importance of relevant agencies working together is an underpinning principle established in the legal framework for children's services. It has been restated in relation to child protection in the consultation paper *Working Together to Safeguard Children: New Proposals for Inter-agency Co-operation* (Department of Health 1999), where the specified agencies are social services, health, education, police, probation and the voluntary sector.

Reder *et al.* (1993: 71) suggest that the issues of responsibility and accountability in respect of children at risk make relationships between disciplines less cooperative:

> Our own experience is that closed professional systems arise in a number of ways. For example, workers may be so conscientious that they are unable to take a step back, and instead resolutely continue with the same focus. Furthermore, the stress of child protection work can drive staff to seek allies to share their anxieties or confirm their beliefs. Some workers hold a passionate conviction that their views are right, so they become even more dogmatic when challenged by possible alternatives.

This demonstrates how anxieties produce defences such as denial and projection, which might make it difficult to consider alternative perspectives and courses of action. Enabling others to contain anxiety, lower their defences and engage in a problem solving dialogue is very important, when difficult courses of action have to be agreed between departments as diverse as the police, social services, health and the family practitioner. It is easy to project blame for what is not going well on to other agencies, rather than to stand back reflectively, take responsibility appropriately and agree cooperatively about what is possible. Likewise, awareness of the creative tension of differing perspectives and roles is needed to avoid collusion, since this may also lead to poor decision making.

Tensions about the provision of care in the community can exist in adult services work between medical practitioners, social workers, relatives and users. The personal skills of the worker are necessary in these situations to achieve the best outcome. Adults with ill-health or disabilities, and those with mental health problems, also need a well coordinated interdisciplinary approach if their needs are to be met holistically, and tragedies avoided. Children and adults are put at risk when professionals fail to communicate and work together. Therefore:

- Although professionals are employed in different sectors, with different responsibilities, there are considerable overlaps in bodies of knowledge, understandings and overall aims. Since counselling skills are used by a wide range of professionals, they can be a unifying factor, offering a common language and approach.
- Interdisciplinary research and training have a crucial role in developing attitudes and experiences of cooperation and the sharing of skills.
- Knowing who should be involved is only the first stage in working towards providing a seamless interdisciplinary service. An attitude of bridge building where commonalities are established by explicit linkages in knowledge, understandings, training and purposes can best mobilize resources for the consumer. Counselling skills can be used to make this happen.
- Social workers with a heritage of working from a breadth of professional knowledge bases are ideally placed to act as brokers

and coordinators for clients. Their underpinning counselling skills can assist the communication and the effectiveness of professional judgements.

Murphy (1993) usefully considers the communication issues in multidisciplinary working and writes: 'as practitioners, we value our interpersonal skills but do not always extend them to our colleagues.' He reminds the reader of the need for:

- listening, giving attention to colleagues;
- valuing the opinions and contributions of others;
- respect for the contributions others bring;
- recognizing stress in others and ourselves;
- willingness to ask questions;
- recognizing structural blocks to communication;
- exploring differences of opinion.

Using these basic counselling approaches with colleagues, as well as carefully following procedural guidelines, helps in decision making and clear communication between agencies.

Specialist counselling services

It has been argued that counselling skills are useful to social workers in fulfilling their tasks in their own organizations and in inter-agency work. This section considers the specialist roles of social workers in some organizations where more advanced skills are needed. A few key thematic areas are covered here, but there are many settings where social workers can make an effective contribution through providing counselling. The client is often best helped by immediate assistance, rather than experiencing delay before referral to expensive and distant services. It is helpful if social workers in advice and intake services can offer brief counselling input to resolve immediate difficulties. Workers in specialized agencies obviously need further advanced skills relevant to their particular area of practice.

Adoption and fostering

The involvement of social workers in the sensitive area of transferring parental rights from one set of adults to another and/or placing children temporarily in the care of others requires high levels of counselling skills. Adoption and post-adoption work means helping individuals to adjust to some complex situations. A full account can be found in Jacobs (1985: 15–20; 1996). Some areas are: the loss and guilt felt by birth mothers and fathers who make the difficult decision that someone else may be in a better position to bring up their child; the adjustments that the adopters need to make to 'owning' their adopted child, and handling their guilt and/or gratitude or other feelings towards the birth parents; the issues for the child, such as feelings about 'being given up', identity issues and curiosity about birth families. Specific work is undertaken in relation to tracing or not tracing birth parents and the varied reactions involved. Local authorities are legally obliged to provide such services, and these and others in the voluntary sector are staffed by specially trained social workers who have specific kinds of knowledge and sensitivity and advanced counselling abilities.

Child abuse

All child abuse work requires sensitive handling. Social workers in children's services in local authorities are trained to work with child protection issues and are offered specialized in-service training to enable them to work with children who have experienced physical, emotional and/or sexual abuse and neglect. Examples given earlier show workers using their counselling skills to enhance this work. Some of these workers have undergone training in more advanced interviewing skills, to enable them to interview children who will give evidence in court when perpetrators have been charged with offences. Most social workers are undertaking work weighted towards disclosure of abuse and the court process.

Children do not always at this stage have the opportunity of specialized therapeutic help. Some social workers, however, are employed in voluntary agencies which offer this. There has also been an expansion in telephone counselling services for children, aiming to give the young people control of the process and choice about referral to direct services. There is similarly a need to work with adults and older people about childhood experiences, which requires specialist counselling expertise. Child and family guidance services and other therapeutic units employ social workers who have undertaken post qualifying therapeutic training to enhance their work.

Learning disabilities

There has been increased recognition of the need to enhance the choice and life opportunities of adults and children described as having learning disabilities. New ideas about communicating and understanding have taken the work forward, carefully considering ways of reducing power differentials and genuinely creating therapeutic encounters in which the user's voice is heard. Brandon (1989) has produced a very useful reader entitled *Mutual Respect*, which explores the ways in which such counselling can usefully take place, including verbal, music and art therapies.

Hospices, death and dying

Social workers are employed in health settings alongside counsellors, occupational therapists and medical specialists. Some of these workers are primarily involved in practical matters and care planning; others have a more therapeutic, counselling role. However, this is an unreal distinction, because in caring for the whole dying or bereaved person, a unique set of needs for emotional and practical assistance is present. Those working in these settings are trained to a more advanced level about bereavement counselling, feelings and attitudes to death and dying, awareness of their own feelings and the impact of the work on themselves. They need advanced skills to faciliate their own work and also the skill to refer to appropriate counselling services as needed. The voluntary sector undertakes much of this specialist work, especially hospices, services for parents whose children have died and services for parents and children who are seriously ill or dying. There are also specialist services for parents whose babies are stillborn or die in unexplained 'cot death'.

Disasters and crises

Local authorities in partnership with health, police and other services have carefully worked out plans to respond to emergencies such as rail or air crashes. Social workers are often designated to join the team of caring professionals who will assist the survivors and shocked relatives at the scene and afterwards. This kind of work requires warmth, compassion and the ability simply to 'be there', and a knowledge of the effects of trauma and post-traumatic stress counselling. The long-term effects on people involved in shock or crisis are well documented. Social workers are often the chosen confidants of people struggling with difficult life events, simply because they are there and the service is visible. Sometimes social workers are already involved with a family when a violent incident or tragic accident occurs. In this capacity they will find themselves at least involved in brief counselling, for which particular skills are needed.

Alcohol and substance use

Working with people who use substances is central to current practice. This is particularly so for workers in mental health and child and family teams. It is a large contributing factor to offending and an important part of probation work. All social workers need a basic understanding of the issues involved in alcohol and drug usage, and when they become harmful to the individual or family. They need to be aware of the research that has linked certain counselling styles to better outcomes. For example, the use of cognitive approaches with offending behaviour has been found the most helpful. Many social workers are employed in specialist agencies which counsel and advise on problem drinking or the control of drug use. Some advanced post-qualifying knowledge and counselling skills training in specific approaches is needed.

Summary

These are only some of the areas where social workers need general counselling skills to facilitate their work, and need to be offered more advanced training in specific areas. Social workers are also involved in fertility and genetic counselling, mental health settings, termination of pregnancy and HIV and AIDS counselling. Much of the work of social workers in these areas takes place in interdisciplinary teams where care is coordinated and methodologies are shared. More work needs to be done on exactly which counselling styles might be most useful in each situation to avoid the unnecessary duplication of approaches to achieve this consumer feedback is essential.

Conclusion

Working in the varied organizational structures which employ social workers requires many skills, from balancing authority in large bureaucracies to learning to be autonomous about the care of individuals in small agencies. Extending the use of counselling skills in good communication with colleagues as well as clients greatly facilitates the professionalism needed to operate flexibly and effectively in a range of organizations.

Chapter **7**

To develop professional competence: relevant counselling skills

It is crucial for social workers to demonstrate their ability to take responsibility for their own learning and professional development. Although many roles and tasks are procedurally led, with clear guidelines to follow, there is still considerable scope for professional discretion. The methods for achieving goals in intervention rely on the worker's ability to select the appropriate tools and to work with clients ethically and responsibly. As adult learners, social work trainees and practitioners contribute to their own development and practice, while supported by managers and peers. Thus, qualifying workers have to demonstrate that they can:

> Manage and evaluate their own capacity to develop professional competence.
>
> (CCETSW 1995)

This means being able to: use supervision effectively; agree priorities and manage their own work schedule; process and administer information well; respond to unexpected opportunities and problems in a professional manner; make decisions when needed; know when to take advice; contribute to the maintenance, critical evaluation and development of their own professional practice; know when they are stressed and take advice; be able to contribute to group discussion; identify and question their own values and prejudices and the implications for practice; handle complexity; resolve dilemmas; negotiate with others; be ethical; and use research to inform practice.

Commitment to professional development for the self and others remains essential for social workers throughout their careers. Post-qualifying and advanced award courses are designed to build on qualifying training and to enable candidates to reappraise their abilities in relation to complex work and the facilitation of the learning of others. Additionally, all practitioners need to keep abreast of changes in the law, new research findings and the implications of all this for practice in agencies. The fast pace of change in recent years makes this particularly important.

The focus of this chapter is on the experience of supervision which is central to any worker's professional development. Supervision enables the worker to: check out that the work is undertaken in a way that is appropriate to the service user and the agency; be given assistance as needed about different, better or more appropriate ways of working; receive support with any particular issues the work is raising; receive assistance with any issues that need to be dealt with in a different part of the agency or in another organization.

Student social workers usually receive regular supervision of an hour and a half weekly. Training programmes specify this in the placement agreement drawn up before the placement with the agency begins. Courses for practice teachers provide guidance for this aspect of their work. It is a sad reflection on present day social work that this might be the only really satisfactory supervisory experience that some practitioners experience. This is of particular concern, since a primary function of supervision is to enable the worker to provide the service user with the best possible service and to protect potentially vulnerable adults and children from worker exploitation. Failure of agencies to support and supervise workers adequately fails primary clients, whose practitioners are not, perhaps, being provided with the opportunity to explore better ways of working with them or options of additional resources. All practitioners should expect to participate in regular planned supervision, and some social workers do experience high-quality support and management in this way.

Supervision in social work has similar antecedents to supervision in counselling practice. Both have a history that includes understandings of the process from a psychodynamic perspective. In both settings the idea of a more experienced person working with a less experienced person is common. In social work this is often the person with responsibility for the management of the supervisee's work, although this is less favoured in counselling settings.

A seminal account of supervision in social work is given by Kadushin (1997), who reviews the literature and history of supervision in public welfare in the USA from 1920 onwards. He comments on the most recent developments:

> The balance between the administrative, educational, and supportive components of supervision has varied widely over the course of the last eighty years. While educational supervision, teetering toward therapy, was in the ascendancy during the 1920s and 30s, more recently the administrative aspects of supervision have moved center stage, especially with the continuing development and diversification of public welfare during the 1950s and 60s.
>
> During the period of intensified concern with social action on the part of social workers in the 1960s and early 1970s there was a reaction against supervision generally. Sensitivity to the rights of all oppressed subordinate groups carried over to the supervisee as an oppressed group. Freedom from supervisory control, a greater emphasis on participatory democracy, and mutuality in the supervisory relationship were given greater emphasis (Mandell 1973).
>
> Growing concern with accountability in the 1970s intensified an emphasis on the administrative aspects of supervision, which is further accented by the 'discovery' and growing interest in burn out which has put greater emphasis on the supportive components of supervision.
>
> (Kadushin 1997: 14)

Kadushin's work on supervision and consultation in itself provides encyclopaedic coverage of its roles and functions. Additionally, there is a substantial literature available to the supervisor in Britain. Two of the most useful and influential are Hawkins and Shohet (1989) and Morrison (1993), who define the functions of supervision as:

- management;
- education;
- support;
- mediation.

Also useful, because it addresses the supervisory concerns of a wide range of agencies, including fieldwork, daycare, voluntary sector, social services and a range of user groups, is Pritchard (1995). In her introduction she writes:

> I have been very fortunate both as a student and as a practitioner always to have had regular supervision of a high standard. I know this is rare; many workers and managers do not regard supervision as important and do not make it a priority. I have seen the consequences of workers not having supervision and of situations in which colleagues have 'done their own thing'. In these times of high stress and low morale, supervision is crucial for all workers.

Another publication aimed at meeting the needs of supervisors in specific aspects of social work is *Staff Supervision in Child Protection Work* (Richards *et al.* 1990). One of a series, published by the National Institute for Social Work, this text reiterates that supervision has four key functions: management, support, education and mediation. The authors expand on them as follows:

> Texts on supervision traditionally quote three major functions of supervision (Kadushin 1997).
>
> - *The management function*: ensuring agency policies and practices are understood and adhered to; prioritising and allocating the work; managing the workload; setting objectives and evaluating the effectiveness of what is done.
> - *The educational function*: helping staff to continue to learn and develop professionally, so that they are able both to cope with societal and organisational demands and to initiate fresh ways of approaching the work, according to changing needs.
> - *The supportive function*: enabling staff to cope with the many stresses that the work entails.

We would add a fourth function, given the rapid pace of change and the need to work collaboratively with other agencies and professionals, particularly in work concerned with child protection. There is a powerful need for *mediation*, whether this is to represent staff needs to higher management, to negotiate what services need to be coordinated, or to clarify to others outside the agency the legal or resource constraints within which the team is operating. This capacity to act as a representative for the team and to enable others to participate in service delivery has become a crucial role for the first line manager and supervisor.

(Richards *et al.* 1990: 14)

The functions and history of supervision in social work are therefore made clear in the literature, with management and mediation increasingly the focus. Additionally, although it is not specified, there is a large element of both *assessment* and *appraisal* within these functions, because the line manager may be the person who supervises and appraises staff, and writes references should they apply for other posts. Thus, where a supervisor combines these functions with that of team leader, the task of supervision is complex and onerous, especially if all the dimensions are to be adequately realized. There is therefore a strong argument for other arrangements to supplement supervision, for personal support and education, such as peer support or group discussion.

This may be partially why, despite a substantial body of knowledge about supervision and increasing pressure of work and need, the delivery of supervision appears to be patchy in social work departments. The gap between knowledge and practice in this area seems wide, contrasting starkly with counselling practice, where detailed and close supervision of practitioners on all levels is considered essential. My own evidence for this comes anecdotally from ex-students and meetings with practice teachers, and also from research studies which comment on the shortfall of good quality experience of supervision for social workers.

Marsh and Triseliotis (1996a: 1) write:

Newly qualified staff have major problems establishing their practice. Induction courses are poor and in-service courses are rarely tailored to their needs. 25% of new staff in social services report that they have no supervision in their first year, and for many others it is unplanned and erratic.

Cleaver and colleagues (1998: 40) write:

> Neither practical tools nor extra training will lead to better decision making if social workers are having to work with an infrastructure which is not supporting them. The overview published by the Department of Health . . . of research programmes noted the variable quality of the supervision received by social workers and the frequency with which inexperienced staff had to deal with difficult situations alone.

In practice, few managers appear to receive special training in supervision skills, despite the models available to them. Ability to supervise relies heavily on 'apprenticeship', in which new supervisors are just as likely to pass on oppression and poor practice as empowerment and good practice. Where practice is competent, no doubt it will be modelled and transmitted, but this seems a very crucial area of managerial activity to leave to such a hit and miss approach.

Inspection reports have frequently identified poor supervision for beginning and inexperienced workers in some local authorities. The opportunity to consult and talk through practice issues regularly and in a structured way with an experienced manager is essential for professional development.

Practice example

In this account a practitioner is described undertaking a piece of work in which constructive supervision was available and helpful. Counselling skills were used to facilitate both the work and the process of the supervision sessions. The worker, in a criminal justice setting, was working with Jason. There were two tasks to complete. First, a court report about the client was prepared. Second, after a 12-month probation order was made, work with Jason was undertaken to address factors that contributed to his offending patterns.

To understand Jason and plan the work, the practitioner considered his situation in the context of Hardiker and Barker's (1988: 40) three levels of analysis:

1 *Structural*: an understanding of inequalities and how they are reinforced through social class, gender, age, disability, ethnicity and regional difference.
2 *Organizational*: in terms of needs and resources and their distribution in relation to personal difficulties, and the way in which social work intervention helps people to access available resources.
3 *Interactional or psychosocial*: in terms of the way in which private difficulties can be understood as influenced by structural as well as personal forces.

In supervision, together with the manager, three strategies related to this analysis were identified: to challenge the offending behaviour; to help Jason to make changes; to help him to move towards a more constructive lifestyle.

Jason's background was that he had grown up 'in care' and had been left with many subsequent unmet needs. He presented the worker with an agenda about caring and controlling. The practitioner had been a care worker before becoming qualified, as a result of which reflecting on his own experience in that setting informed his understanding of Jason. The worker thought about the client's experiences of inconsistency in residential and foster care since he was 14. The practitioner's previous professional background knowledge, as a residential care worker, meant that he concluded that Jason's life had been truly both disadvantaged and disrupted.

Knowledge of the negative effects of care influenced the practitioner's objectivity. Therefore, when the report was written, too much detail was included in the first draft. Supervision proved invaluable to analyse and discuss the issues the case raised, and to make sure that the report presented to the court included only what was relevant to securing the appropriate disposal. However, issues remained, and the practitioner commented that 'it is impossible to separate entirely the social worker's self and personal style from the process of the work.'

Thus the worker supervised the order flexibly in relation to national standards because of a first-hand knowledge of the inadequacy of residential care in preparing people for their future lives. This was discussed with the supervisor, and knowledge of the care system was used to look at the client's history of being moved around, and the impact this had on his current lifestyle and inability to settle. It was concluded that he had emotional and practical problems which originated from his care history, and that this could be substantiated by drawing on research findings about the outcomes for young people leaving the public care system, not just from personal experience.

The client had now become a parent himself, but was out of work and expressing frustration with housing and the benefits agency. He was acting out his dissatisfactions through offending. The dilemma for the worker was how to build a constructive, supporting relationship while at the same time adopting an authoritative role. The latter was inevitable because of the threat of breach should Jason fail to comply with the restrictions of national standards for offenders on orders. The role of social control is explicit in surveillance and rehabilitation. The practitioner looked at the literature which argues that these roles can be combined without diminishing either, and also at that which argues against such a perspective, in order to help to achieve the aims within the setting. This professional role issue of accountable care and control on behalf of society was explored in supervision.

Through contract-based task-centred work the supervisor helped the practitioner to combine the roles, using state-imposed *boundaries* to structure and focus the work. The client could not just opt out, but the window of opportunity to create change was fleeting and precarious. This made the skill of the worker in seizing the opportunity more important. *Resistance* was frequently expressed through *silence* and withdrawal, despite overt compliance. The effectiveness of role combination depended upon the personal skills of the worker.

This worker also relied upon *'the intuitive use of the self'* because of past associations with the care system. 'Jason not only needed my practical support, he also needed me to recognize and respond to his experiences.' *Warmth* and *genuineness* were offered in an open relationship, while *clarity about the boundaries* and structural aspects was maintained. In this struggle between sympathy and *empathy*, the worker found that 'my own professional supervision proved invaluable in allowing space and time to reflect on these issues.'

The agreed plan was to work on accommodation, employment, relationships, self-image and confidence. The practitioner used interpersonal skills to work in a cognitive behavioural way and did some task-centred work on the practical issues, finding that 'a concerned and genuine relationship is necessary for change', but was also active, directive and challenging, as the supervising role required.

Supervision had already assisted the worker with management and education. Now supervision was a support to the worker in maintaining a complex programme, particularly when a waiting room incident, beyond the worker's control, led to Jason exploding verbally in reception because he felt humiliated by something that was said to him. The supervisor helped the worker to debrief his own feelings, and use the incident to work with Jason on his inner feelings. The supervisor acted as mediator, resolving the matter within the office context satisfactorily. Much of the subsequent work focused on the client's sense of worthlessness. His anger was recognized as the beginning of a change that needed to be built into assertiveness.

During the task-centred work around accommodation, the worker met the *defences of reluctance and avoidance*. Jason would agree to act and then fail. For example, the council was willing to allocate a flat but Jason would fail to turn up to view it. He then took the keys, failed to view and failed to return the keys. The worker was reluctantly pushed into going with him to secure a tenancy. The worker felt that this resistance and sabotaging of achievement in his life needed to be *confronted*, as he did not keep appointments with GPs, employment agencies or alcohol advice. Thus his 'worthlessness' found its outlet in anger and passive hostility, not in confidence and assertion.

This link was made retrospectively in supervision. The worker commented that 'I had not recognized that Jason needed a lot more support in achieving an independent life. He was capable of carrying out the tasks but lacked motivation and the confidence to do so. I believe I expected too much of Jason and it would have been more empowering to try and work to smaller more manageable tasks which could have been more easily achieved and therefore more likely to build his confidence. This knowledge has come retrospectively, but has illustrated to me the value of constantly reflecting on how my work is developing, and making changes accordingly.'

This worker believed in Jason's capacity for change. He wanted his own home and job and 'a normal life'. Throughout life the client had been consistently faced with inequalities, unemployment, homelessness and discrimination because of his appearance, lack of education and social and family networks. He obtained a flat and began to see that his negative thoughts about himself could change. This process was contained by a genuine and structured relationship, a combination of caring and professionalism. It was time-consuming but productive. The worker's honesty, knowledge and skills, together with effective reflective and managerial supervision, enabled the practice to develop and change. The analysis of the client's resistance avoided the simplistic device of labelling or blaming him for his lack of confidence to act. The holistic view of him based on an understanding of his background, agency constraints and social inequalities proved an effective analytical and planning tool. The supervisor provided an environment where there was trust and openness in the supervisory relationship to facilitate learning, and where the worker felt safe to explore the impact of work on self, through support, management, education and mediation.

Training for supervision

Some training of a basic nature is offered to practice teachers, who often use their practice teaching as a ladder to management posts. There seems to be an unchallenged assumption that anyone promoted to management also has the ability to supervise the work of others. While new supervisors should have practice skills which enable them to build useful supervisory relationships, and the knowledge to facilitate others to fulfil their professional tasks, much is assumed, without corroborative evidence. Who supervises the supervisors?

The tools needed to supervise others include management ability, clarity about agency goals and practices, knowledge of the law and substantial practice experience. Alongside this, however, it is important to have the ability to contain and allow ventilation of anxieties about the work. These, if left unresolved, reduce workers' coping mechanisms and contribute to stress and sickness. This ability includes the basic counselling skills described for practice, but also more advanced understandings of power dynamics, and the defences and resistances that affect worker performance.

Supervision in social work practice is clearly neither psycho-therapy nor a personal support system for the practitioner. But given that any feeling human being is likely be affected by the nature of the work, then listening, responding, checking and empathic support by managers all remain important. Likewise, if errors are to be avoided in complex cases, some understanding of how workers may deny or distort their understandings under pressure seems essential. Whatever the model adopted, personal communication skills are needed to facilitate process. Workers need time to reflect upon and analyse decision making and the personal components of their responses.

Hawkins and Shohet (1989: 77–9), in their chapter on super-visor training and development, offer a self-assessment ques-tionnaire for supervisors. Their major headings are: knowledge;

supervision management skills; supervision intervention skills; traits or qualities; commitment to own ongoing development; group supervisor skills; senior organizational supervisor skills. This is a useful inventory which provides a good baseline for assessing training needs. Time out to reflect on practice along these lines is crucial for managers.

The literature on supervision also offers ideas for moving away from reliance on hierarchical one-to-one supervision. While management responsibility has to remain in its appropriate organizational place, peer and group support arrangements could be used more to allow ventilation and debriefing of feelings, as well as exchange of skills. This is a process already informally in operation in many offices. To recognize this process formally and dedicate time to it would assist managers and staff alike.

Supervision courses are an essential component of management training, and need to offer practical as well as theoretical teaching. While the comprehensive literature delineates tasks, roles and functions, less attention is given to how supervisors might combine functions with skills of communication and intervention. It has been demonstrated through research (Dickson and Bamford 1995) that such interpersonal skills are improved through practice. Supervision is a key area for the application of counselling skills so that the management, education, support and mediation functions of supervision are served effectively.

Courses in supervision and mentorship can offer managers the opportunity to reflect on and build on skills. For example, the Leicester University School of Social Work Post Graduate Certificate in Supervision and Mentorship (Child Care) by Distance Learning enables participants to: 'appraise critically a wide range of theories and models of supervision, mentoring and management'. The course literature states:

> First line managers/supervisors are essential in the provision of children's services, as has been highlighted by inquiry and inspection reports and more recently in the Department of Health publication Child Protection: Messages from Research . . . They need a sound knowledge base, high quality interpersonal and communication skills, the ability to manage individuals, teams, budgets and resources as well as change, conflict and stress. CCETSW's post qualifying

framework requires that supervisors also possess skills in staff development and appraisal and that they continually update their knowledge base.

Consultation

Supervisors, however well trained they are, cannot be experts in everything. Opportunities to use the expertise of consultants, in a non-managerial role, can be useful to supervisors in building their knowledge base and offering expertise in respect of particular issues. This way of increasing the educational abilities of first-line managers appears to be less used than it might be, except perhaps in legal matters. Regular access to consultants on specific issues is an effective way of delivering ongoing in-service training to managers who supervise others.

Counselling for staff

Supervision, however well delivered, cannot provide everything that workers need if the day-to-day demands of stressful work precipitate other personal issues. Counselling is established in societal thinking as useful in supporting people in terms of crisis or personal change. Recently, this view has been challenged in the press, with writers suggesting that stress is positive, or that counselling creates a dependency culture, of which the only good outcome is more jobs for counsellors (Gordon 1995: 23). While counselling is no panacea, and is unnecessary for those whose inner resilience, personal support systems or other interests sustain them, there are none the less times when the emotional support of a professionally trained counsellor with no personal agenda is helpful.

It is clearly recognized in counselling literature and training that the experience of 'being helped' is part of the development of the ability to help. There is therefore no stigma attached to being a client, although this does not seem to be the case in the hierarchical approach to helping which sometimes appears in social work. There also appears to be a culture in some social work environments whereby social workers are expected to survive with few supervision sessions, and no other accredited personal support, despite the amount of work, time pressures and the stressful nature of much of the work undertaken.

It seems sad that a profession with a clear set of values, knowledge and skills for practice views the ability of workers to seek assistance with complex work, or personal support, not as maturing and strong, but as a weakness. This issue is discussed from time to time in the professional journals. For example, Dougan (1996: 12):

> As a social worker who has attended a variety of workshops over the years and is now in training as a therapist, I have been continually struck by the absence of other social workers on courses which often included teachers, nurses and other professionals.
>
> This is largely to do with the often abusive environment that is endemic in many social services departments.
>
> There appears to be a notion that seeking counselling is a sign of professional weakness. In my view the opposite is likely to be the case.

It is also apparent that helping professions attract those whose personal histories have given them insights into some of the difficulties faced by clients. This can be an excellent motivator, but it is not surprising if, from time to time, the personal nature of much social work triggers a personal reaction in the helper. Training assists beginning practitioners to look at their personal values and the impact of the work on them. Even the most experienced worker will be emotionally affected by the work. In some situations it would be surprising if any worker could be unaffected. One of the workers with the West family, dealing with the aftermath of sadism, abuse and murder, wrote:

> Eventually the children were found permanent placements and the care team's task came to an end . . . The personal cost was high. All of us felt we would never be the same again. We had gone around for so long with all this information locked in our heads and we were unable to let it out. You felt you could never be normal again . . .

> We were all offered counselling and many of us are
> still receiving it. We have group sessions where it is a real
> relief to be able to say anything you want and know that
> no one will be shocked or upset by it.
>
> (West Social Worker 1996)

The nature of social work is such that stress and burn-out
have become more common. Agencies facing escalating costs
from absence and retirement due to stress and ill-health in the
workforce need to address the human needs of their workers.
Writing in *Community Care*, North (1996) quotes a manager as
saying: 'the pressure of caseload management means a lot of
time previously available to discuss the issues of a particular case
and also the effect on the social worker has been squeezed and
we have lost the time to deal with personal issues.' In the same
article she continues: 'It came as no surprise that months after
the launch of council's employee assistance programme this
summer, social services staff have become its biggest users.'
Such schemes show belated recognition of the stress that social
workers face, and reflect the way in which supervision has
become almost wholly managerial. Workers need another service
to meet the outcomes of increasingly complex work and the
impact of hostility and violence from the public. However, where
such schemes are available, it has to be recognized that the agency
context has an input to what is offered. As Carroll and Walton
(1997: 1) remind us about counselling in organizations,

> Counselling is never private. Personal yes. Private no. Even
> when confidentiality is negotiated clearly, even when these
> two individuals (counsellor and client) meet regularly alone,
> the context in which they meet and the contexts to which
> they return once they have met, influence what happens
> between them . . . the counselling room is filled with other
> individuals and systems, groups and organisations that are
> part of the lives of both participants.

They offer a helpful checklist for organizations considering employee counselling services (Carroll and Walton 1997: 2):

1 How will the organization view those who come for counselling
  – officially and unofficially?

2 Will involvement in counselling affect careers?
3 Who in the organization will know which people have been for counselling?
4 Will counselling be used by managers to get rid of people, to give them bad news, punish them or get them to conform?
5 What information about clients will be shared with whom?
6 How will the organization receive feedback from the counselling service?
7 Will the counsellor(s) be seen as part of the organization and how will this affect their credibility?
8 What will happen if counsellors have divided loyalties between the client and the organization?

These kinds of questions reflect the fears and anxieties of employees approaching an employment based service with legitimate, work-related issues. It is therefore essential that these issues, mainly around confidentiality and future employment prospects, are openly and publicly resolved at the outset. The benefits of a completely confidential service to employees along the lines of student health services in universities might be the most empowering way to assist with worker stress. As Walsh (1987: 283) suggests,

> All human systems, indeed all humans, can profit from periodic reflection on their behavior with the help of the perspective of a third party. Many mental health and social service professionals spend considerable time playing just such a consulting role for others; we should accept its value for ourselves as well.

While it is important that employers provide such schemes to workers to alleviate stress by offering support and counselling services at times of personal work-related crisis, both as a matter of right and on a confidential basis, these should not be seen as a substitute for addressing working practices on a day-by-day level. Strategies that help include formalizing and disseminating employee rights; respecting employee rights; ensuring that workers take their holiday entitlement each year and claw back unpaid overtime promptly; providing good information; making space for team meetings and support groups; facilitating workshops and further training.

The process of regular supervision should be reliable, and designed not only to ensure that work is done properly, but also to check that stress does not remain unaddressed. The front-line worker should be able to expect skilled support and assistance at the point where the work itself makes the greatest impact. Supervision needs to provide the four elements of support, education, mediation and management, underpinned by an accepting and boundaried approach.

Conclusion

Counselling practice, as much as the management ethos, has much to offer social workers in developing their own professional competence. There is helpful literature on managing workplace stress (Nucho 1988; Cartwright and Cooper 1997). Nucho's book is particularly useful in considering the self as operating in five domains: transpersonal, achievement, interpersonal, body, mind. All these aspects of personality are engaged in social work practice, and the book is helpful in its holistic approach to the practitioner.

Developing professional competence engages the whole person in a range of functions which are the concern of professional employers. Supportive supervision, one-off consultations on difficult work, personnel initiatives and relevant in-service training are all elements that enable practitioners to meet these requirements.

Chapter 8

Counselling skills for relationship, competence and good outcomes

I began by clarifying the differences between counselling and the use of counselling skills to facilitate social work processes. I have considered each of the six core qualifying competences, how these are derived from social work's body of knowledge about theory and method, and the ways in which counselling skills are used by social workers to undertake their tasks. I conclude by asserting the importance of human interpersonal skills to carry out caring tasks holistically as well as accountably. I argue that:

- relationships remain at the heart of effective practice;
- the ethic of valuing and respecting others underpins both counselling and social work practice;
- there is still a need for social work based on sound process and facilitated by good interpersonal skills;
- work undertaken in relation to life transitions and crises means that social workers need to be equipped for supportive counselling roles;
- practitioners show the usefulness of counselling skills in their day-to-day practice;
- research into effective practice supports these messages.

Relationships remain at the heart of effective practice

Biestek's *The Case Work Relationship* was published in 1961. Younghusband, a leading figure in social work education, wrote in the introduction that 'attempts to analyse the nature of relationships between persons and the use of this relationship by the social worker are beset with pitfalls'. Biestek himself wrote: 'a conceptual understanding of the relationship does not automatically give skill in establishing and using it; skill can be developed only through repeated intelligent practice. As in all human endeavours, however, understanding can be an aid in acquiring skill; knowing the elements of a good relationship may be the first step toward skill' (Foreword). Biestek sets out and develops six principles which have been highly influential ever since: individuation; purposeful expression of feelings; controlled emotional involvement; acceptance; the non-judgemental attitude; client self-determination and confidentiality.

The professional relationship does appear to be a contradiction in terms, yet it remains the conduit for the delivery of services in social work, health care, education, the legal profession and other human service professions. This is evidenced by the range of professional people who find counselling courses useful for their work, including doctors, nurses, teachers, care workers, undertakers, roadside rescue services, sales personnel and tax advisors. A counselling skills approach to ethical communication provides a sound basis for a range of professional practice. In human transactions, use of the relationship cannot be ignored. Counselling, psychosocial casework and other interpersonal exchanges can be facilitated by skills training.

Social work has always operated on the basis of professional relatedness, and practitioners work with people at a time of life crisis or acute stress. Service users can be very vulnerable and exposed, challenging and hostile, very ill, socio-economically disadvantaged or oppressed. Whatever the structure of the organization for the delivery of services, social work relies on a high degree of person-to-person contact by telephone and interview. This transaction is between people with differing levels of power and influence. The social worker is in a professional role, with the ability to give or withhold services. The user is seeking assistance or has been compelled to seek it. Other personal dimensions, such as gender or 'race', may affect this transaction (see Chapter 2). The worker is the one mandated by agency function to mediate in the life space of another.

The Department of Health (1996: 4) stated that, 'In social services more than in many other professions, personnel at all levels can have sustained one to one contacts with vulnerable clients.' The nature of the transaction makes it particularly important that ethical, boundaried, non-stigmatizing, enabling, yet warm, empathic and accepting relationships are offered by social care staff to people in their care or on their case loads, using ethically based skills. The skills of relationship are the foundation from which other functions are built, so that where trainees do not meet these first requirements adequately it is difficult to contemplate how they can operate at all. As we have seen, most transactions in social work practice require communication skills of a high order, with the ability to engage all users in an enabling way. This is recognized in the requirements for advanced and post-qualifying awards.

Counselling has been criticized for a preciousness about 'the relationship'. Social work has been similarly castigated. Workers involved with children who died at the hands of carers have been considered to have elevated the relationship with the adults to the detriment of the child, a perception which changed subsequent childcare practice. Social work and counselling relationships must have the right boundaries, and should only be entered into in order to achieve an ethical and agreed purpose. It is also important to select the appropriate people with whom to engage, and to be aware of the potential for both collusion and abuse, especially if promoting the rights of one party curtails the rights of another possibly less powerful person. This dilemma of whose needs and rights should be promoted is a key ethical issue in social work which does not arise often in counselling, where one-to-one confidential relationships are usual. In social work the practitioner has to handle a series of complex interrelationships: parent, child, grandparent, user, carer, offender, society. There are therefore potentially competing agendas and the ethic of confidentiality is exercised differently.

Social work has been criticized for becoming over-bureaucratic and concerned with organizational aims at the expense of the wishes of consumers and workers. Joyce Brand (1997) wrote an article in the *Independent* which sums up the frustrations of many practitioners:

> I finally and sadly abandoned social work when Shropshire joined London and the rest of the South East in discarding genuine personal involvement with people needing help in favour of mechanistic rituals designed to protect the organisation. I am not alone – more than 80 workers in one local authority have taken early retirement this year.

In her article, she describes the nature of the human and helping encounters of her earlier working experience:

> I had never before failed to maintain my optimism and enthusiasm despite the heart aching task I had often to perform – what could move any woman more than to hear a young mother dying of cervical cancer describe what she wants for her children when she is no longer with them. I have heard the painful revelations of a small child whose body has been abused, and I have seen that pain shared and that child helped by the social worker.

Good organization, administration, procedural guidelines and policies are essential to competent social work practice. Efficient administration, easy to handle forms, clear guidelines and policies are an essential part of caring. They can facilitate action, ease dilemmas and save precious time. Importantly, they help to make the worker accountable, ensure more equitable service distribution, protect the service user from potentially abusive hidden actions and avoid the misuse of individual discretion by workers.

However, a reaction to the conflicts of competing demands, high caseloads and dwindling resources can be that social workers take refuge in bureaucracy. It is therefore important to question too much preoccupation with agency routines at the expense of high-quality service to users in terms of relationship. To focus entirely on the agency agenda flies in the face of the well articulated call from users for supportive relationships from social workers.

The debate about the competence model in social work training has produced other artificial dichotomies. Competent practice does not mean mechanical disregard of process; neither can competence in social work simply be a series of assessable observed behaviours. Jones and Joss, writing about models of professionalism, show that it is possible to build a matrix of competences from which the reflective practitioner can assemble holistic, structured sets that inform the exercise of professional discretion. This includes process and interpersonal/interaction skills (Yelloly and Henkel 1995: 31).

Professional relationships and personal competence remain at the heart of effective social work practice. They form the core of service delivery, whatever the legal, organizational or procedural context. Public confidence is not maintained when this aspect is neglected. At the National Association for Practice Teaching conference (1996), two of the keynote speakers reasserted this in different ways. Statham, from the National Institute for Social Work Education, addressed the future of social work education. The key themes presented were:

- learning to manage change;
- working in partnership across agencies;
- learning to learn;
- learning to be flexible;
- the re-emergence of relationship and process in social work.

An argument was made for developing a style of relationship looking not just at the roles and tasks of social work, but also at how things are done and the quality of relationships in social work interactions. Dominelli (1996), in a complementary address, argued that in understanding the relationship between client, society and ourselves we discover what social work is, how it should be taught and assessed. This analysis of the continuities and discontinuities of the history of the social work profession put relationships back at the heart of competent practice for the future.

In the following year (1997) this theme was developed in a conference that addressed the 'place of people, the process and outcomes in social work education'. In the workshop introduction, England (1997: 3) said that the conference title: 'assumes social work should above all be person centred; it reflects a widespread feeling that social work and social work education have become too impersonal and too instrumental. Such developments are thought to be inimicable to social work.' The challenge to social work education and practice is to integrate a personal and relationship-oriented service with accountable organizational procedures and mandates. The achievement of this balance in a professional, focused, reflective and humanistic way is the key to a holistic service in which professionals, the public and policy makers may have confidence.

The ethic of valuing and respecting others underpins both counselling and social work practice

As discussed above, all transactions between people need boundaries framing what is or is not permitted behaviour. These are designed to enhance personal security and confidence about the limits of power and to deter exploitation and abuse. CCETSW has defined a set of values for the guidance of social work trainees at qualifying and post-qualifying levels. They are to demonstrate in their practice that they:

- identify and question their own values and prejudices and their implications for practice;
- respect and value uniqueness and diversity, and recognize and build on strengths;
- promote people's rights to choice, privacy, confidentiality and protection, while recognizing and addressing the complexities of competing rights and demands;
- assist people to increase control and improve the quality of their lives, while recognizing that control of behaviour will be required at times in order to protect children and adults from harm;
- identify, analyse and take action to counter discrimination, racism, disadvantage, inequality and injustice, using strategies appropriate to role and context;
- practise in a manner that does not stigmatize or disadvantage individuals, groups or communities (CCETSW 1995).

The British Association for Social Work publishes 12 principles for social work practice that are concerned with positive use of knowledge, skills and experience for the good of the community and individuals.

- knowledge, skills and experience used positively for the benefit of all sections of the community and individuals;
- respect for clients as individuals and safeguarding their dignity and rights;
- no prejudice in self, nor tolerance of prejudice in others on grounds of origin, race, status, sex, sexual orientation, age, disability, beliefs or contribution to society;
- empowerment of clients and their participation in decisions and defining services;
- sustained concern for clients even when unable to help them or where self-protection is necessary;
- professional responsibility takes place over personal interest;
- responsibility for standards of service and for continued education and training;
- collaboration with others in the interests of clients;
- clarity in public as to whether acting in a personal or organizational capacity;
- promotion of appropriate ethnic and cultural diversity of services;
- confidentiality of information and divulgence only by consent or exceptionally in evidence of serious danger;
- pursuit of conditions of employment which enable these to be respected.

I quote these in full because the ethical dimensions of social work practice always feature in day-to-day work and decision making. Ethical insights and values perspectives inform the resolution of competing agendas, especially where the law may be uninterpreted. This ethical concern is reflected in the nature of the relationship between user and practitioner and the outcome in service delivery. Codes of ethics are therefore helpful, but subject to reappraisal in the light of changing societal definitions of social problems.

Social workers, when qualified, operate from professional codes which the public expect them to honour. One of the difficulties in counselling and psychotherapy has been the unregulated nature of some therapists' practice. The British Association for Counselling came into existence to address this. It publishes detailed ethical and procedural guidelines for counsellors which are, in their main concerns, congruent with social work values. For the purposes of brokering services, practitioners need to check, or advise users to ask for, the guidelines from which agencies and individuals practise to safeguard their consumers. Unethical counselling practices need challenging as much as does poor social work practice. Care needs to be taken to evaluate the credentials of some 'counselling agencies' and 'counsellors', whose training and experience may be limited, and accountability not scrutinized. In the contracting culture of modern social work practice it is important that:

- purchasers of counselling services are knowledgeable in their quality control of what is purchased;
- individual workers are able to use their own counselling skills within practice to good effect, while consideration of referral is ongoing;
- individual workers are aware of the range and limits of their own expertise in counselling skills;
- individual workers know of the accredited sources of more skilled counselling or psychotherapeutic assistance for clients;
- individual workers know about specialized counselling resources, such as debt counselling or Relate, to which service users can be referred;
- individual workers know enough to give good information to clients seeking counselling, to be able to assist clients to avoid manipulation or abuse.

The ethical statements of CCETSW, as well as those of BAC and BASW, go a long way to ensuring that there is a frame of reference for ethics in social work and counselling practice. However, responsibility remains with organizations and individuals to make these reality, and to examine contested areas carefully.

The need for a social work based on good process facilitated by sound interpersonal skills is still evident

Social work process is about how social workers carry out the tasks they are expected to undertake. This may be defined as a 'series of interactions between clients and practitioners', which involves 'cycles of assessment, intervention and evaluation, in which goals are identified, methods used and resources mobilised' (Seden *et al.* 1996).

These processes are a fundamental and enduring feature of social work, from its early beginnings in the poor law to the present day, and can be seen in many areas of practice. Community care practice is about assessments of need, followed by packages of care, evaluation and further assessment or case closure. Children and family practitioners assess the needs of children, intervene by providing services or taking other action, then evaluate. Criminal justice workers follow similar cycles of practice in gathering information for reports, carrying out plans to reduce offending behaviour and evaluating outcomes. Most voluntary agencies assess whether a client is to receive a service, deliver the service and then evaluate. These cycles of social work activity take place within complex legal, organizational, ethical and resourcing boundaries of acceptable practice. How these events are achieved is related not only to structural issues, important as these are, but also to the interpersonal skills and resourcefulness of the individual worker.

This is the key reason why professional social work cannot be undertaken by administrators, volunteers or untrained streetwise grannies. Professional social work is a welfarist alternative to more intrusive controlling interventions, such as custody or institutionalization, and relies on effective and ethical process from a workforce skilled in managing people and resources humanely. Social work process based on interpersonal skills has high potential value and function for society, in managing deprivation, deviance, abuse, injustice and malfunction in the social system. This role of intermediary between the public and government is very important and requires a high quality of process to be effective. If service users lose confidence in the ability of the profession to broker between personal needs and the state in a person-centred and process conscious way, social work practice as it is known will become marginalized. As Statham (1996) asserts, 'recovery of the importance of process in human interactions revitalises the social care process.' She continues:

> managers are increasingly recognising the importance of process and style in achieving change. Similarly, service

users, carers and their organizations say that it is the style
of the worker, the relationship and their ability to spend
time working with them which is valued.

Work undertaken in relation to life transitions and crisis means that social workers need to be equipped for supportive counselling roles

Social workers find themselves acting in other people's lives at
all stages in the life cycle, because difficulties or crises can occur
for individuals at all points. Babies can be wanted, not wanted or
abused. Parents can need support and/or services in respect of a
child's disability or illness. Growing children and their families
may be referred to social workers in respect of their care, educational needs or behaviour. Adolescent young people may meet
social workers when in conflict with parents or society, or when
society has failed them. Young, middle-aged and older adults
come into contact with social workers through parenting, offending, disability, bereavement, illness, employment rights, nation-
ality issues or benefit issues, and for many other reasons. While
the focus of this book has been on examining how counselling
skills facilitate practice in the most usual social work contexts,
it is also the case that in many of their activities social workers
use advanced counselling skills and undertake counselling roles.
Some examples are counselling in relation to matters such as
abuse, adoption, alcohol abuse, bereavement, disability, drugs,
HIV and AIDs, offence reduction and parenting, as examined in
Chapter 6.

Life cycle literature is relevant to both counsellors and social
workers. It provides a research-led knowledge base for understanding what reactions and behaviours are within normal limits, and
what factors help people to manage their lives more creatively
and satisfactorily within their own beliefs, communities and cul-
tures. Both counsellors and social workers consider issues of attachment, transition and loss as core elements in their helping work.
Social workers rarely undertake long-term therapeutic personal
work, but are often the initial point of help for families and individuals in a time of stress or crisis. Social workers need sufficiently
good counselling skills to undertake this crucial initial response.

Practitioners demonstrate the usefulness of counselling skills in their everyday practice

Reference was made in Chapter 1 to a survey of practitioners across a range of social work settings, who use counselling skills in their daily social work activities. At the end of the questionnaire the practitioners were invited to make any additional comments they thought relevant. One person said it was important to say that the skills learned on the counselling programme were relevant to the whole range of work in a busy child protection team. Another childcare practitioner wrote that counselling training had been a major impetus in the post-qualifying development of her practice. Another, in relation to a particular piece of work, said: 'I feel strongly that it was the relationship built as a result of the use of counselling skills that made progress possible in spite of the authoritarian monitoring which I also had to carry out as the key worker for the children.'

A practitioner with experience of working with adults in a local authority field work team said that all the counselling skills learned were useful with people. Basic skills were used to facilitate tasks, but more advanced skills were also helpful, such as containing anxiety, working with transference and countertransference, linking experiences, interpreting and understanding behaviours. One adult services-based worker said that counselling skills were helpful in a team support role, and another that 'the use of skills related to context and linked to problem solving and goal setting was very relevant to social work practice.' Finally, a very experienced worker wrote:

> Since the Community Care Act the social work task with adults has been seen as assessment and setting up packages of care. In my experience often a relationship tangle had to be dealt with before the assessment could proceed. The use of a wide range of counselling skills was needed to formulate the moving forward of assessment.

These practitioners articulated the efficacy of using counselling skills to facilitate their primary work and process in a way that did not lose sight of the agency's primary goal of service delivery or social work values, and which was effective in agreed interventions.

Research into effective practice supports these messages

Since the spate of legislation giving a new focus to mandates for social work intervention (Children Act 1989, Community Care and NHS Act 1990, Criminal Justice Act 1991) there has been much research to evaluate the implementation of legislation at the point of delivery in social work agencies. While the primary focus of such research has not been counselling skills, one outcome which recurs is thematic reference to counselling skills and personal support to facilitate interventions. This is illustrated briefly from three studies which consider the implementation of new legislation in local authorities.

Hardiker and Barker (1996) examined the implementation of the Community Care and NHS Act in one large county and city social services area. They systematically interviewed commissioners, carers, providers and users in relation to 24 cases of needs-led assessment and care management. The user groups included older people, disabled, learning disabled and mental health referrals. The primary outcome was to show social workers using existing values, knowledge and skills in a time of rapid agency change and development to meet the requirements of new legislation.

When the researchers examined the work methods chosen, they found that what they termed 'counselling/casework' was rated highly. The body of the report showed case management and assessment facilitated by counselling skills. For example, in one not untypical case,

> The social worker provided counselling including:
> - listening and engaging him in constructing his own plan;
> - helping him to manage anxiety and stress regarding job applications and interviewing;
> - helping him to reconstruct his negative views of his own performance;
> - helping him to build a realistic relationship with his parents;
>
> The user participated in all parts of the plan. His parents were impressed by the care shown by the workers, and were very satisfied with the outcome.
>
> (Hardiker and Barker 1996: 34)

In relation to the 24 cases, the researchers commented that 'social care planning, casework and counselling were central approaches to meeting need and managing the transitions the users needed to make', and that:

> Many of the users had long-term needs, and their disabilities were often serious, with the prospect of deterioration. Some were isolated, and living narrow and restricted lives (often shared by their carers). In many cases their living arrangements were at a point of change . . . Sometimes their support networks and interactions were at risk.
>
> These factors led to a considerable amount of stress, in both users and carers. Some were very distressed, and needed the opportunity to express their grief and fears about the future.
>
> (Hardiker and Barker 1996: 23, 24)

Hardiker and Barker (1994) undertook similar research in relation to the implementation of the Children Act (1989), examining in depth a purposive sample of 12 families where the thresholds for significant harm were assessed as met. This study showed that counselling skills remained a key method of intervention, alongside decisive action to protect children and support families.

Aldgate and colleagues researched the contribution of respite care (temporary planned accommodation) to family support for children in need. They were able to examine the outcome of services provided to families in several local authorities, chosen to represent divergent populations and geographical areas. The main purpose of the study was to look at the use and efficacy of respite services. The report considers the application of family support services to a particular group of children and their families, and identifies the components of the services that contributed to successful outcomes for the children and families interviewed. The study shows that the provision of respite is successful in 60 per cent of the cases and quantifies the ways in which social work processes facilitated this. One factor in achieving success for families was the use of counselling skills in casework interventions. The researchers write about the importance of social work support:

What emerged during the study was the complex role of the family support social worker as complete case managers, integrating the activities of social care planning and social casework. Not only did social workers organise the service but they undertook direct work with parents, identifying problems and together seeking strategies to ameliorate them. Carers were co-opted into these strategies when appropriate, for example to advise parents on improving their parenting skills or to make children feel special. Throughout the placement, the family support social worker kept in touch with parents by letter or phone to monitor the progress of the placement. In short they engaged in the classic social work processes of assessment and intervention which are best described as social casework. This professional relationship was valued and used by clients to good effect.

(Aldgate and Bradley 1999: 206)

It was also clear from this study that the counselling skills of workers were used to facilitate the classic processes of intervention, managing the transition and ending the contact positively. When needed, skills in interviewing parents, carers and children were used to facilitate this process. The use of skills to broker community networks which could exist into the future was also crucial.

An important finding from the study was how social isolation could be improved, first through the intervention enabling parents to build links with extended family and second, through the development of links into the community via the carers. The social work input in this study was crucial in effecting a positive outcome for parents and children.

(Aldgate and Bradley 1999: 204)

Conclusion

This recent research, the voices of users and carers, the evidence of social work educators, the current political agenda of social inclusion and the cases presented in this book all combine to reflect and affirm the use in social work process of interpersonal skills for enabling and sustaining personal contacts. This is usually with temporarily or more permanently vulnerable people seeking assistance with some troubling aspects of their lives. Social workers are often asked to intervene when others have tried to help and have not succeeded. Thus they are entrusted by society with demanding and complex tasks. To achieve success, sound inter-personal skills are needed. The range and scope of social work tasks mean that if the more advanced counselling and com-munication skills are used, within current legislative mandates, to facilitate classic social work processes of assessment, intervention and evaluation, practice competence in social care is considerably enhanced.

Appendix   Skills for empowerment in social work

Power to be acquired over	Social work activity – access	Social work activity – support	Social work skills required for activity
1 *Resources* e.g. Income, Housing, Support Services, Transport.	Enabling influence over current and future services by access to decision makers. Allowing advocates to act on behalf of clients.	*Developing themes* – Assisting users to make a link between personal and social issues. For example, poor housing (social issue) and family functioning (personal issue).	Listening Empathy Advocacy
2 *Relationships* Relationships with professional staff who provide services.	Offering clients choices about the services they use. Offering clients methods and support in making complaints about the service.	*Evaluating self-image* – Assisting users to revive self-confidence and self respect. *Defining and selecting problems* – Helping users to define their own problems and avoid definitions made for them by professionals.	Empathy Respect Counselling Negotiation Advocacy Empathy Respect, Counselling
3 *Information* Giving information about services and their standards.	Giving information to clients about service offered. Setting standards for services so clients know what to expect.	*Becoming aware of policies* – Assisting users to become aware of the services and resources that exist and assisting as part of an educational and political process.	Anti-oppressive practice Advocacy

4 Decision making The way decisions are made and by whom and in what settings.	Offering places to clients on decision making bodies. Enabling influence over current and future services by access to decision makers.	*Developing and using choices* – Helping users recognize that choice is available and recognize what might be possible.	User involvement in negotiation
		Experiencing solidarity with others – Bringing users together to share and develop confidence, trust and solidarity.	Empathy and respect
		Acquiring and using language – Helping users develop language that allows them to make connections between one context of power and another.	Advocacy
		Resisting a return to a state of powerlessness – Helping clients not to return to familiar positions of powerlessness (i.e. a return to an institution or a situation of domestic violence).	Counselling Anti-oppressive practice
		Developing interactive and political skills – Helping clients to learn through action and reflection on action towards achieving specific objectives.	Negotiation and conciliation
		Evaluation – Helping users examine the objectives of empowerment and where necessary to redefine the objectives and strategies to achieve them.	Advocacy Listening

Source: Neville 1996

References

Abbott, A. (1995) Boundaries of social work or social work boundaries?, *Social Services Review*, December, 546–62.

Aldgate, J. and Bradley, M. (1999) *Supporting Families through Short Term Fostering*. London: HMSO.

Allen-Meares, P. and Lane, B. A. (1987) Grounding social work practice in theory: ecosystems, *Social Casework: the Journal of Contemporary Social Work*, November, 515–21.

Bamford, D. and Dickson, D. (1995) Improving the interpersonal skills of social work students: the problem of transfer of training and what to do about it, *British Journal of Social Work*, 25, 85–105.

Barnes, R. (1990) The fall and rise of casework, *Community Care*, 12 July, 822.

Bateman, N. (1995) *Advocacy Skills*. Aldershot: Arena.

Beardshaw, V. (1991) *Implementing Assessment and Care Management*. London: Kings Fund College Paper.

Berne, E. (1961) *Transactional Analysis in Psychotherapy*. New York: Grove Press.

Biestek, F. P. (1961) *The Casework Relationship*. London: George Allen and Unwin.

Bird, G. (1997) Letter, *Community Care*, 25 September.

Bowlby, J. (1988) *A Secure Base: Clinical Applications of Attachment Theory*. London: Routledge.

Bradshaw, J. (1972) The concept of need, *New Society*, 30 March, 640–3.

Brand, J. (1997) Letter, *Independent*, 19 April.

Brandon, D. (ed.) (1989) *Mutual Respect*. Surbiton: Hexagon Publishing.

Braye, S. and Preston-Shoot, M. (1995) *Empowering Practice in Social Care*. Buckingham: Open University Press.

Breakwell, G. (1990) *Interviewing*. London: Routledge.

Brearley, J. (1991) *Counselling and Social Work*. Buckingham: Open University Press.

British Association for Counselling (1984) *Code of Ethics and Practice for Counsellors*. Rugby: British Association for Counselling.

Browne, M. (1996) Needs assessment and community care, in J. Percy-Smith (ed.) *Needs Assessment in Public Policy*. Buckingham: Open University Press.

Caplan, G. (1964) *Principles of Preventative Psychiatry*. New York: Basic Books.

Carroll, M. and Walton, M. (eds) (1997) *Handbook of Counselling in Organizations*. London: Sage.

Cartwright, S. and Cooper, G. L. (1997) *Managing Workplace Stress*. London: Sage.

CCETSW (1995) *Rules and Requirements for the Diploma in Social Work (Revised)*. London: CCETSW.

Cleaver, H., Wattam, C. and Cawson, C. (1998) *Assessing Risk in Child Protection*. London: NSPCC.

Cochrane, D. (1990) Power, probation and empowerment, *Probation Journal* 36(4) May: 177–82.

Compton, B. R. and Galaway, B. (1989) *Social Work Processes*. Pacific Grove, CA: Brookes Cole.

Corby, B. (1996) Risk assessment in child protection, in H. Kemshall and J. Pritchard (eds) *Good Practice in Risk Assessment and Risk Management*. London: Jessica Kingsley.

Corey, G. (1997) *Theory and Practice of Counselling and Psychotherapy*. Pacific Grove, CA: Brookes Cole.

Cornwall, N. (1980) Who directs the power in talking with clients?, *Social Work Today*, 28 September, 17–18.

Coulshed, V. (1991) *Social Work Practice: an Introduction*. London: Macmillan.

Curnock, K. and Hardiker, P. (1979) *Towards Practice Theory: Skills and Methods in Social Assessments*. London: Routledge and Kegan Paul.

Dalgleish, L. I. (1997) Risk assessment approaches: the good, the bad and the ugly, Paper presented to the Sixth Australasian Conference on Child Abuse and Neglect, 20–24 October, Adelaide, South Australia.

Dalgleish, L. (in press) *Risks and Decisions in Child Protection*. Chichester: Wiley.

Dalgleish, L. I. and Drew, E. C. (1989) The relationship of child abuse indicators to the assessment of perceived risk and to the court's decision to separate, *Child Abuse and Neglect*, 13, 491–506.

Davies, D. and Neal, C. (1996) *Pink Therapy*. Buckingham: Open University Press.

Davies, M. (1985) *The Essential Social Worker*. Aldershot: Arena.

Deakin, N. (1996) Contracting and accountability: the British experi-ence, in H. J. Schulze and W. Wirth (eds) *Who Cares? Social Service Organizations and Their Users*. London: Cassell.

Department of Health (1991a) *Assessment Systems and Community Care*. London: HMSO.

Department of Health (1991b) *Care Management and Assessment: Practi-tioners Guide*. London: HMSO.

Department of Health (1996) *The Obligations of Care*. London: HMSO.

Department of Health (1999) *Working Together to Safeguard Children: New Government Proposals for Inter-agency Co-operation*. London: HMSO.

Department of Health (2000) *Framework for the Assessment of Children in Need and their Families*. London: The Stationery Office.

de Shazer, S. (1985) *Keys to Solution in Brief Therapy*. New York: Norton.

de Shazer, S. (1988) *Investigating Solutions in Brief Therapy*. New York: Norton.

Dickson, D. and Bamford, D. (1995) Improving the inter-personal skills of social work students: the problems of transfer of training and what to do about it, *British Journal of Social Work*, 25, 85–105.

Doel, M. and Marsh, P. (1992) *Task-centred Social Work*. Aldershot: Arena.

Dominelli, L. (1996) Address, NOPT Conference, University of Leicester, 11–13 September.

Doueck, H. J., Bronson, D. B. and Levine, M. (1992) Evaluating risk assessment implementation in child protection: issues for consid-eration, *Child Abuse and Neglect*, 16, 637–46.

Dougan, T. (1996) Counselling can add to the benefits of experience (letter), *Community Care*, 18 January, 12.

Dowie, J. and Elstein, A. (eds) (1988) *Professional Judgement: a Reader in Clinical Judgement Making*. Cambridge: Cambridge University Press.

Doyal, L. and Gough, I. (1991) *A Theory of Human Need*. London: Macmillan.

Eaton, L. (1998) How long have we got?, *Community Care*, 4 June, 18.

Egan, G. (1990) *The Skilled Helper*. Pacific Grove, CA: Brooks Cole.

England, H. (1997) 'Where have all the people gone?' National Organ-ization for Practice Teaching (NOPT) Conference, Manchester Uni-versity, 9–11 July.

English, D. and Pecora, P. (1994) Risk assessment as a practice in child protection services, *Child Welfare*, 53, 451–73.

Erikson, E. (1965) *Childhood and Society*. Harmondsworth: Penguin.

Fairbairn, W. R. D. (1952) *Psychoanalytic Studies of the Personality*. London: Routledge and Kegan Paul.

Franklin, C. and Jordan, C. (1995) Qualitative assessment: a methodo-logical review, *Families in Society*, May, 281–95.

Gandhi, P. (1996) When I'm sixty four: listening to what elderly people from ethnic minorities need, *Professional Social Work*, February, 12–13.

Garbarino, J. (1982) *Children and Families in the Social Environment.* New York: Aldine.

Gaudin, J. M., Shilton, P., Kilpatrick, A. C. and Polansky, N. A. (1996) Family functioning in neglectful families, *Child Abuse and Neglect,* 20(4), 363–77.

Golan, N. (1981) *Passing through Transitions.* London: Collier-Macmillan.

Gordon, J. (1995) Counselling, who needs it?, *You,* 22 October, 23–7.

Haines, J. (1975) *Skills and Methods in Social Work.* London: Constable.

Handy, C. (1993) *Understanding Organisations.* Harmondsworth: Penguin.

Hardiker, P. and Barker, M. (1988) A window on childcare, poverty and social work, in S. Becker and S. McPherson (eds) *Public Issues, Private Pain: Poverty, Social Work and Social Policy.* London: Insight.

Hardiker, P. and Barker, M. (1991) Towards social theory for social work, in J. Lishman (ed.) *Handbook of Theory for Practice Teachers in Social Work.* London: Jessica Kingsley.

Hardiker, P. and Barker, M. (1994) *The 1989 Children Act – Significant Harm. The Experience of Social Workers Implementing New Legislation.* Leicester: University of Leicester School of Social Work.

Hardiker, P. and Barker, M. (1996) *The NHS and Community Care Act 1990: Needs-led Assessments and Packages of Care.* Leicester: University of Leicester School of Social Work.

Hasenfield, Y. (1983) *Human Services Organizations.* Englewood Cliffs, NJ: Prentice Hall.

Hawkins, M. and Shohet, P. (1989) *Supervision in the Helping Professions.* Buckingham: Open University Press.

Heron, J. (1997) *Helping the Client.* London: Sage.

Hill, M. and Meadows, J. (1990) The place of counselling in social work, *Practice,* 4(3), 156–72.

Hollis, F. (1964) *Casework: a Psycho-social Therapy.* New York: Random House.

Home Office (1997) *Management and Assessment of Risk in the Probation Service.* London: HMSO.

Home Office (1998) *Report of the What Works Project: Strategies for Effective Offender Supervision.* London: Home Office Publications.

hooks, b. (1991) *Yearning: Race, Gender, and Cultural Politics.* New York: Turnaround Books.

Howe, D. (1987) *An Introduction to Social Work Theory.* Aldershot: Wildwood House.

Hudson, B. L. (1991) Behavioural social work, in J. Lishman (ed.) *Handbook of Theory for Practice Teachers in Social Work.* London: Jessica Kingsley.

Hudson, B. L. and MacDonald, G. M. (1986) *Behavioural Social Work: an Introduction.* London: Routledge.

Hugman, B. (1977) *Act Natural.* London: Bedford Square Press.

Humphries, B. (ed.) (1996) *Critical Perspectives on Empowerment.* London: Ventura.

Inskipp, F. (1986) *Counselling: the Trainer's Handbook.* Cambridge: National Extension College.

Jacobs, M. (1982) *Still Small Voice.* London: SPCK.

Jacobs, M. (1985) *Swift to Hear.* London: SPCK.

Jacobs, M. (ed.) (1995a) *Charlie: an Unwanted Child?* Buckingham: Open University Press.

Jacobs, M. (ed.) (1995b) *Jitendra: Lost Connections.* Buckingham: Open University Press.

Jacobs, M. (1996) *The Care Guide.* London: Cassell.

Jacobs, M. (1998) *The Presenting Past.* Buckingham: Open University Press.

Kadushin, A. (1997) *Supervision in Social Work.* New York: Columbia University Press.

Keith-Lucas, A. (1972) *Giving and Taking Help.* Chapel Hill: University of North Carolina Press.

Kemshall, H. and Pritchard, J. (1996) *Good Practice in Risk Assessment and Risk Management.* London: Jessica Kingsley.

Lago, C. and Thompson, J. (1996) *Race, Culture and Counselling.* Buckingham: Open University Press.

Laird, J. (1995) Family centred practice in the postmodern era, *Families in Society*, March, 150–62.

Lhullier, J. M. and Martin, C. (1994) Social work at the turn of the century, *Social Policy and Administration*, 28(1), 359–69.

Lindsey, D. (1994) *The Welfare of Children.* Oxford: Oxford University Press.

Lipsky, M. (1980) *Street Level Bureaucracy.* New York: Sage.

Lishman, J. (1991) *Handbook of Theory for Practice Teachers in Social Work.* London: Jessica Kingsley.

Lloyd, M. and Taylor, C. (1995) From Hollis to the orange book, *British Journal of Social Work*, 25(6), 691–707.

Lyons, P., Wodarski, J. S. and Doueck, H. J. (1996) Risk assessment for child protective services: a review of the empirical literature on instrument performance, *Social Work Research*, 20(3), 143–55.

McGuire, J. (ed.) (1995) *What Works: Reducing Offending. Guidelines from Research and Practice.* Chichester: Wiley.

Maluccio, A. (ed.) (1981) *Promoting Competence in Clients: a New/Old Approach to Social Work Practice.* New York: The Free Press.

Mandell, B. (1973) The equality revolution and supervision, *Journal of Education for Social Work*, 9, 43–54.

Marsh, P. and Triseliotis, J. (1996a) Abstract of *Ready to Practise? Social Workers and Probation Officers: Their Training and First Year in Work.* London: HMSO and Scottish Office.

Marsh, P. and Triseliotis, J. (1996b) *Ready to Practise? Social Workers and Probation Officers: Their Training and First Year in Work.* Aldershot: Avebury.

Mayer, J. E. and Timms, N. (1970) *The Client Speaks*. London: Routledge and Kegan Paul.

Mearns, D. and Thorne, B. (1988) *Person Centred Counselling in Action*. London: Sage.

Meyer, C. H. (1993) *Assessment in Social Work*. New York: Columbia University Press.

Millar, W. R. and Rollnick, S. (1991) *Motivational Interviewing*. London: Guildford Press.

Moore, W. (1997) Speak to me before it's too late, *Health Service Journal*, 2 January, 20–2.

Morrison, T. (1993) *Staff Supervision in Social Care: An Action Learning Approach*. Harlow: Longman.

Murphy, M. (1993) *Working Together in Child Protection: an Exploration of the Multi-disciplinary Task and System*. Ashgate: Arena.

Murphy Berman, P. (1994) A conceptual framework for thinking about risk assessment and case management in child protective services, *Child Abuse and Neglect*, 8(2), 193–201.

Nelson-Jones, R. (1981) *Practical Counselling and Helping Skills*. London: Cassell.

Neville, D. (1996) Empowerment: Learning and Teaching in Practice. Unpublished PhD thesis, University of Leicester.

North, S. J. (1996) Stress, *Community Care*, 30 October, 20–1.

Nucho, A. O. (1988) *Stress Management*. Springfield, IL: Thomas.

O'Hagan, K. P. (1986) *Crisis Intervention in Social Services*. London: Macmillan.

Payne, M. (1992) *Modern Social Work Theory: a Critical Introduction*. London: Macmillan.

Pearson, G., Treseder, J. and Yelloly, M. (1988) *Social Work and the Legacy of Freud*. London: Macmillan.

Percy-Smith, J. (ed.) (1996) *Needs Assessments in Public Policy*. Buckingham: Open University Press.

Perlman, H. H. (1957) *Social Casework*. Chicago, IL: University of Chicago Press.

Pincus, A. and Minahan, A. (1973) *Social Work Practice: Model and Method*. Itasca, IL: Peacock.

Pittman, F. S. (1966) Techniques of family crisis therapy, in J. Masserman (ed.) *Current Psychiatric Therapies*. New York: Grune and Stratton.

Powell, J. and Goddard, A. (1996) Cost and stakeholder views: a combined approach to evaluating services, *British Journal of Social Work*, 26, 93–108.

Prins, H. (1995) Seven sins of omission, *Probation Journal*, 42(4), 199–201.

Pritchard, J. (ed.) (1995) *Good Practice in Supervision*. London: Jessica Kingsley.

Rapp, C. A. (1996) The Strengths Model: Case Management with People Suffering from Severe and Persistent Mental Illness. Unpublished manuscript, University of Kansas.

Reder, P., Duncan, S. and Gray, M. (1993) *Beyond Blame: Child Abuse Tragedies Revisited*. London: Routledge.

Reid, W. J. (1963) An experimental study of methods used in casework treatment, PhD Dissertation, Columbia University, New York.

Reid, W. J. and Epstein, L. (1972) *Task-centred Casework*. New York: Columbia University Press.

Reid, W. J. and Epstein, L. (1976) *Task-centred Practice*. New York: Columbia University Press.

Reid, W. J. and Shyne, A. W. (1969) *Brief and Extended Casework*. New York: Columbia University Press.

Richards, M., Payne, C. and Shepperd, A. (1990) *Staff Supervision in Child Protection Work*. London: NISWE.

Richmond, M. E. (1922) *Social Diagnosis*. New York: Russell Sage Foundation.

Roberts, A. P. (1995) *Crisis Intervention and Time Limited Cognitive Treatment*. London: Sage.

Roberts, R. W. and Nee, R. H. (1970) *Theories of Social Casework*. London: University of Chicago Press.

Rogers, C. R. (1961) *On Becoming a Person*. Boston: Houghton Mifflin.

Rosenstein, P. (1995) Parental levels of empathy as related to risk assessment in child protective services, *Child Abuse and Neglect*, 19(11), 1349–60.

Rutter, M. (1985) Resilience in the face of adversity: protective factors and resilience to psychiatric disorder, *British Journal of Psychiatry*, 147, 163–82.

Rutter, M., Taylor, E. and Hersov, L. (1994) *Child and Adolescent Psychiatry: Modern Approaches*, 3rd edn. Oxford: Blackwell.

Ryan, M., Foot, J. and Hawkins, L. (1995) From beginners to graduate social worker: preliminary findings of an Australian longitudinal study, *British Journal of Social Work*, 25, 17–35.

Ryle, A. (1995) Cognitive analytic therapy, in M. Jacobs (ed.) *Charlie: an Unwanted Child?* Buckingham: Open University Press.

Saleeby, D. (1997) *The Strengths Perspective in Social Work Practice*. New York: Longman.

Schaffer, R. H. (1990) *Making Decisions about Children: Psychological Questions and Answers*. Oxford: Blackwell.

Schon, D. (1983) *The Reflective Practitioner*. New York: Basic Books.

Scott, D. and O'Neill, D. (1996) *Beyond Child Rescue: Developing Family Centred Practice at St Lukes*. St Leonards: Allen and Unwin.

Scrutton, S. (1989) *Counselling Older People*. London: Arnold.

Seden, J., Hardiker, P. and Barker, M. (1996) Child protection revisited: balancing state intervention and family autonomy through social work processes, *Child and Family Social Work*, 1(1), 3–12.

Seligman, M. E. P. (1975) *Helplessness: On Depression Development and Death*. San Francisco: W. H. Freeman.

Sheldon, B. (1982) *Behaviour Modification: Theory, Practice and Philosophy*. London: Tavistock.

Sinclair, R., Garnett, L. and Berridge, D. (1995) *Social Work and Assessment with Adolescents*. London: National Children's Bureau.

Siporin, M. (1975) *Introduction to Social Work Practice*. New York: Macmillan.

Smith, M. (1991) *Analysing Organisational Behaviour*. London: Macmillan.

Smith, S. and Norton, K. (1999) *Counselling Skills for Doctors*. Buckingham: Open University Press.

Solomon, B. (1976) *Black Empowerment: Social Work in Oppressed Communities*. New York: Colombia University Press.

Sone, K. (1996) Professional roles, *Community Care*, 21–27 November, 19.

Specht, H. and Vickery, A. (1977) *Integrating Social Work Methods*. London: George Allen and Unwin.

Statham, D. (1996) Address, NOPT Conference, Leicester University, 11–13 September.

Taylor, B. and Devine, T. (1993) *Assessing Needs and Planning Care*. Aldershot: Arena.

Taylor-Gooby, P. and Lawson, R. (eds) (1993) *Markets and Managers: New Issues in the Delivery of Welfare*. Buckingham: Open University Press.

Thompson, N. (1995) *Aging with Dignity*. Ashgate: Arena.

Townsend, J. (1987) *The Interviewers Pocket Book*. Alresford: Management Pocket Books.

Trowell, J. and Bower, M. (1996) *The Emotional Needs of Young Children and Their Families*. London: Routledge.

Truax, C. B. and Carkhuff, R. R. (1967) *Towards Effective Counselling and Psychotherapy*. Chicago: Aldine.

Wald, M. and Woolverton, M. (1990) Risk assessment: the emperor's new clothes?, *Child Welfare*, 69, 483–8.

Walsh, J. A. (1987) Burnout and values in the social service profession, *Social Casework: The Journal of Contemporary Social Work*, May, 279–82.

West Social Worker (1996) After West, *Social Work*, January, 10.

Whalley, M. (1994) *Learning to Be Strong: Setting up a Neighbourhood Service for Under Fives and Their Families*. Sevenoaks: Hodder and Stoughton.

White, M. and Epston, D. (1989) *Narrative Means to Therapeutic Ends*. New York: Norton.

Williams, B. (1996) *Counselling in Criminal Justice*. Buckingham: Open University Press.

Winnicott, D. W. (1960) The theory of the parent–infant relationship, *International Journal of Psycho-analysis*, 41, 585–95.

Yelloly, M. (1980) *Social Work Theory and Psychoanalysis*. New York: Van Nostrand.

Yelloly, M. and Henkel, M. (eds) (1995) *Learning and Teaching in Social Work: towards Reflective Practice*. London: Jessica Kingsley.

Index